one
more
try

one more try

What to do when your marriage is falling apart

GARY CHAPMAN

MOODY PUBLISHERS

CHICAGO

All Scripture quotations, unless otherwise indicated, are taken from the *Holy Bible, New Living Translation*, copyright © 1996, 2004, 2007 by Tyndale House Foundation. Used by permission of Tyndale House Publishers, Inc., Carol Stream, Illinois 60188. All rights reserved.

Scripture quotations marked NASB are taken from the *New American Standard Bible®*, copyright © 1960, 1962, 1963, 1968, 1971, 1972, 1973, 1975, 1977, 1995 by The Lockman Foundation. Used by permission. (www.Lockman.org)

Scripture quotations marked ESV are taken from *The Holy Bible, English Standard Version*. Copyright © 2000, 2001 by Crossway Bibles, a division of Good News Publishers. Used by permission. All rights reserved.

Scripture quotations marked NIV are taken from the *Holy Bible, New International Version®*, *NIV®*. Copyright © 1973, 1978, 1984, 2011 by Biblica, Inc.™ Used by permission of Zondervan. All rights reserved worldwide. www.zondervan.com.

Edited by Elizabeth Cody Newenhuyse   Cover design: Smartt Guys design
Interior design: Ragont Design   Cover photos: Shutterstock
Author photo: P.S. Photography

Previously published as *Hope for the Separated*

Library of Congress Cataloging-in-Publication Data
Chapman, Gary D.
  [Hope for the separated.]
  One more try : what to do when your marriage is falling apart / Gary Dr. Chapman.
      pages cm
  Summary: "When doors slam and angry words fly, when things just aren't working out, and even when your spouse has destroyed your trust, there is hope. If you feel like your marriage is near the breaking point - even if you have already split up - Gary Chapman will show you how you can give your marriage one more try. Separation does not necessarily mean divorce is imminent. Matter of fact, it's possible that separation may even lead to a restored, enriched, growing marriage. The outcome of this time of transition is determined solely by the individuals involved. If you're willing to make the most of that process, begin the journey with confidence as Gary walks you step-by-step towards healing and hope"-- Provided by publisher.
  Includes bibliographical references.
  ISBN 978-0-8024-1151-8 (paperback)
  1. Divorce--Religious aspects--Christianity. 2. Marriage--Religious aspects--Christianity. 3. Reconciliation--Religious aspects--Christianity. 4. Separated people. I. Title.
  HQ823.C49 2014
  306.81--dc23
                          2014007221

*To the many couples
who, in the pain of marital crises,
accepted the challenge of
seeking reconciliation, and allowed
me to tell of their journeys.*

Contents

introduction

"i can't take it anymore"

Emily was articulate. Too articulate. She had always been clever with words, but now, as she and her husband of fifteen years, Tim, began arguing more frequently, her criticisms cut more deeply. Money. Tim's job issues. The stresses of an adopted child with emotional problems. All this played out against the background of some long-buried childhood hurts.

Feeling bruised and defeated, Tim, more easygoing by nature, began to think, "I can't take this anymore. Is it worth it?" Some of his friends suggested separation. His pastor urged him to stick it out. A counselor he knew said, "You need to take a 'time out' to get yourself healed."

Tim was more confused than ever . . .

Allie twiddled with her phone as she watched TV. She noticed it was getting late, and Zach still wasn't home. She knew his job as catering manager for a downtown hotel required late nights, especially during busy seasons. Still . . . there was more. A distance.

Soon, she found out why.

And who.

Kevin couldn't believe he was hearing these words from his pastor. "Kevin," Pastor Doug said. "You and Tricia have to separate temporarily to save your marriage."

"What? You mean, move out? Leave my kids? Be 'weekend daddy' like a guy I work with?"

"Yes," said the pastor. "I know some of the issues you're dealing with and how the two of you are in constant conflict. I think it's exactly what you need."

Kevin kept protesting, picturing himself in a lonely apartment. But, he admitted to himself, something had to be done. He and Tricia argued all the time—except when she could hardly look at him. Couldn't be good for the kids. Maybe it was worth a try.

All marriages, of course, endure ups and downs. But some need more than a "tune-up" or a weekend away from the kids. Some—like those above—need saving.

More often than not this will require the intervention of a professional therapist. I have devoted many years to helping people with troubled relationships. Many of those who have come to my office entered at the point of marital separation. The stress level in their marriage reached a point where one spouse had walked out. The pain of separation and the real possibility of divorce drove them to seek help.

Others were not yet at the point of walking out, but were considering separation. Either way, they were rapidly losing hope for the survival of their marriage. They were at the point where they "couldn't take it anymore."

Part of my role as a counselor is to provide hope. Whether you are currently living apart or simply feel that your marriage is falling apart, you need to know that you are not alone and that there is hope. You need to know that your marriage is worth fighting for.

> You need to know you are not alone and there is hope.

I won't tell you that this is easy. As one counselor puts it, "It's easy to fall in love, but very hard to fight for love."[1]

In our society, it is also profoundly countercultural. In this book we will explore the reasons why staying together is the better way. We will address honestly what to do when a marriage cannot be saved. We will share stories of couples who brought their marriages "back from the brink."

This book does not contain easy answers or rigid formulas. There is no simple medication for a marriage diseased to the point of separation. But for those who really want help, even if the medicine is hard to swallow, read on. Your chances of recovery are good.

For pastors, lay counselors, and relatives who want to help those in the throes of marital discord or separation, I have sought to give practical, hopeful answers in language that everyone can understand. A number of helpful books have been written for those already divorced, but few, in my opinion, deal adequately with those struggling with separation or contemplating the end of their marriage.

As Kevin heard from his pastor, it is not to be assumed that separation always leads to divorce. Separation may just as well lead to a restored, enriched, growing marriage—but that is an outcome that must be determined by the individuals involved. It also should not be assumed that a marital crisis—the kind where one or both partners feel as if they "can't take it anymore" and seriously consider splitting up—inevitably leads to divorce.

Of course, ultimate value comes not in reading but in applying truth. An ancient sage once said, "The journey of a thousand miles begins with one step."

I hope this book will help you take that step.

1

what happened to our dream?

Julie sat in the outer area of the principal's office, waiting to meet with him. Her son was in trouble—again. This time it was serious. She had texted her husband, Tom, who worked not far from the school. He had written back, "Sorry, big meeting, can't leave." Now she was fuming. Typical Tom, never there when his family needed him. It was a pattern—and Julie was seriously beginning to wonder if she could put up with it much longer.

This couple embodies the reality I speak of in *Desperate Marriages*: the "stone wall" a husband and wife can build between them. Each stone represents an event in the past where one of them failed the other.[1]

Then there's Mike. He had always loved sharing life with Jen, boasting to others that his wife was his "best friend." But now they had a couple of kids, and it seemed Jen threw herself into mothering and didn't have much left for him. Feeling lonely and abandoned, Mike started spending more time at the local sports bar with his buddies. Then he and Jen would argue. And slowly, the stone wall was going up between them.

Some couples can't stop bickering. Everything, it seems,

sparks conflict. They become exhausted to the point of feeling physically ill. They aren't even sure they like each other anymore. Maybe, they reason, they'd be better off apart.

"My father was a very angry man," one woman recalls. "He and Mom fought a lot—he would yell and Mom would react defensively or just shut down. Our household was pretty turbulent, although there were many moments of peace. Would we have been better off if they had split up? Hard to say, and in those days divorce was uncommon. But conflict definitely takes its toll."

A Little Death

If your marriage is marked by more days of conflict than companionship, you might be wondering, "Where did it all go? What happened to the dream of lifelong love and commitment?"

If you are separated, it may feel like a little death. Every day your spouse's absence reminds you of what you have lost. If you are physically together but emotionally estranged, that, too, can feel like something is dying—a dream, a hope. We speak of the "valley of the shadow of death." But a shadow is not to be equated with death itself. Your marriage crisis, separated or not, may be the valley of restoration, and the pain you feel may be the labor pains that will give rebirth to your marriage.

On the other hand, separation may be the beginning of the end. The fruit of your separation will be determined by what you and your spouse say and do in the next few weeks and months.

In a very real sense, a marriage in crisis calls for intensive care, much like that given to one in grave physical danger. The condition of your marriage is "critical." Things can go either way at any moment. Proper medication is essential, which is the purpose of this book. Surgery may be required. That will call for the services of a counselor or pastor. What you do in the next few weeks will determine the quality of your life for years to come. Be assured, God is concerned about the outcome. You can count on Him for supernatural help.

This is not the time to capitulate. The battle for marital unity is not over until the death certificate is signed. The dreams and hopes you shared when you got married are still worth fighting for. You married each other because you were in love (or thought you were at the time). You dreamed of the perfect marriage in which each made the other supremely happy. What happened to that dream? What went wrong? What can you do to correct it?

The dream can live again. But not without work—work that will demand listening, understanding, discipline, and change—work that can result in the joy of a dream come true.

I know some of you are saying, "It sounds good, but it won't work. We've tried before. Besides, I don't think my spouse will even try again."

Perhaps you are right, but do not assume that the hostile attitude of your spouse will remain forever. One of the gifts of God to all men and women is the gift of choice. We can change, and that change can be for the better. Your spouse may be saying, "I'm through. It is finished. I don't want to talk about it!" Two weeks or two months from now, however, your mate may be willing to talk. Much depends on what you do in the meantime, and much depends on his or her response to the Spirit of God.

Others of you are saying, "I'm not sure that I want to work

on this marriage. I've tried. I've given and given. It won't work, and I may as well get out now!" I am deeply sympathetic with those feelings. I know that when we have tried again and again without success, we may lose our desire to try once more. We see no hope, so we conclude that we have no alternative but to give up. Our emotions no longer encourage us to work on the marriage.

> I never ask people, "Do you want to work on your marriage?" I always ask, "Will you work on your marriage?"

That is why I never ask people, "Do you want to work on your marriage?" I always ask, "Will you work on your marriage?" At the point of crisis, we have lost much of our "want to." We must remember our values, our commitments, and our dreams, and we must choose to do what must be done to be true to them.

Where shall we go for help? For those who are Christians, there is one stable source to which we turn when we need guidance. That source is the Bible. Non-Christians may or may not turn to the Bible, but the Christian is drawn by the Spirit of God to the Scriptures. In the Bible, we find not only what we ought to do, but also the encouragement to do it. Even the non-Christian who sincerely seeks help in the Bible can find meaning in Paul's statement, "I can do all things through him who strengthens me" (Philippians 4:13 ESV). When we come to Christ, we find the outside help we need to do what our own resources are inadequate to accomplish.

Wrong Way!

When we turn to the Bible for guidance on marriage, we see two road signs: one marked Wrong Way, the other Detour. On the sign marked Wrong Way appears the word *divorce*. On the sign marked Detour appear the words *marital unity*. Let us explore the meaning and direction of those two signs.

According to the Old and New Testaments, divorce always represents the wrong way. In the beginning, when God told Adam and Eve, "Be fruitful and multiply and fill the earth" (Genesis 1:28 ESV), He never gave the slightest hint that the marital relationship was to be anything but lifelong. The first mention of divorce in the Bible is found in the writings of Moses.[2] Moses permitted divorce, but it was never condoned or encouraged by God. Jesus later explained to the Pharisees that Moses had permitted divorce only because of their "hardness of heart" (Matthew 19:8 ESV) but that from the beginning divorce was not God's plan. Jesus affirmed that God's intention was monogamous, lifelong marital relationships. When God instituted marriage, divorce was not an option. God did not create divorce any more than He created polygamy. Those were human innovations. In God's sight, those innovations are always clearly wrong.

On the other hand, the sign marked Detour—Marital Unity indicates that you have not lost sight of the goal, nor are you off the road. Rather, you are taking the circuitous route of separation because the bridge of your togetherness has collapsed. Marital discord has weakened the marriage bridge, and the path to restored harmony in your marriage is no longer a short, straight route.

The detour sign may bring an immediate feeling of distress, but behind distress lies hope. There are at least signs to point you back to the main route—toward renewed marital unity. If you will follow carefully, the chances of finding your way are good.

Right now, you are standing at a fork in the road of your life. You must choose which path you will follow in the next months. We have seen that God never encourages divorce, but He still allows humankind the freedom to choose either route. In the course of human history, man has made many unwise decisions. God has not immediately destroyed humans for their wrong. Had God chosen that recourse, man would have been extinct thousands of years ago. God has allowed us genuine freedom—including freedom to curse God and walk our own way. The Bible indicates that, to one degree or another, we have all used that freedom to our own undoing (Isaiah 53:6).

> When God says divorce is the wrong way, He is not trying to make life difficult. He is pointing to prosperity and hope.

The principle of human freedom God grants us is stated in Galatians 6:7: "Don't be misled—you cannot mock the justice of God. You will always harvest what you plant." God has simply allowed humanity to reap the harvest from the seed we plant, hoping that humans will learn to plant good seed: "Whoever sows to please their flesh, from the flesh will reap destruction; whoever sows to please the Spirit, from the Spirit will reap eternal life" (Galatians 6:8 NIV).

God's plans for His people are good. God never instituted anything designed to make us miserable. "'For I know the plans I have for you,' says the Lord. 'They are plans for good and not for disaster, to give you a future and a hope'" (Jeremiah 29:11). When God says divorce is the wrong way, He is not trying to make life difficult. He is pointing the way to prosperity and hope.

"But we don't have prosperity and hope," you say. That may be true, but past failure need not dictate the future. The lack of fulfillment you have experienced probably came from one of three sources: lack of an intimate relationship with God, lack of an intimate relationship with your mate, or lack of an intimate understanding and acceptance of yourself. The first and last of those can be corrected without the aid of your spouse. The second, of course, will require the cooperation of both husband and wife. Radical change in all three areas is highly possible. Thus, the potential for the rebirth of your marriage is assured.

In later chapters I will offer ways of initiating change in each of the above areas. But first, I want to state clearly that the biblical ideal for a couple in crisis calls for reconciliation. You may not feel like reconciling. You may see no hope for reunion. The process may frighten you, but may I challenge you to follow the example of God Himself?

Reconciliation and Repentance

Throughout the Bible, God is pictured as having a love relationship with His people—in the Old Testament with Israel and in the New Testament with the church. On many occasions God has found Himself separated from His people, not of His choosing but of theirs. In a sense, the entire Bible is a record of God's attempts to be reconciled to His people. The book of Hosea gives the most graphic picture of the process.

Gomer, Hosea's wife, was unfaithful time and time again, but God said, "Go and love your wife again . . . This will illustrate that the Lord still loves Israel, even though the people have turned to other gods" (Hosea 3:1). In spite of Israel's idolatry and unfaithfulness to God, He said, "But then I will win her back once again, I will lead her into the desert and speak tenderly to her there" (2:14).

In the New Testament we hear Jesus express the pain of separation when He says, "O Jerusalem, Jerusalem, the city that kills the prophets and stones those who are sent to it! How often would I have gathered your children together as a hen gathers her brood under her wings, and you were not willing! See, your house is left to you desolate" (Matthew 23:37–38 ESV).

In the book of Jeremiah, God recalls Israel's devotion in the wilderness and how He protected Israel from her enemies during those days. But then came the coldness, the separation. "Does a young woman forget her jewelry? Does a bride hide her wedding dress? Yet for years on end my people have forgotten me (2:32).

The remainder of the book is a plea for reconciliation: "O Israel, my faithless people, come home to me again, for I am merciful," God entreats His people (3:12).

But God invites His children to "come home" while also correcting their sinful behavior, commanding them to "throw away your detestable idols and stray away no more"

(4:1). There can be no reconciliation without repentance. In the marital relationship there must be mutual repentance, for almost always the failure has involved both parties.

I do not wish to minimize the hurt, pain, frustration, anger, resentment, loneliness, and disappointment you may feel. Nor do I take lightly your past efforts at marital adjustment. Rather, the purpose of this chapter is to call you to accept the challenge to fight for your marriage—and if you are separated, to use this time to grow and learn.

Sometimes separation brings a sense of emotional peace to the individual. That peace is mistakenly interpreted as an indication that separation and divorce must be right. One husband said, "This is the first week of peace I have had in years." Such peace is the result of removing yourself from the scene of the battle. Naturally you have peace; you have left the conflict! Retreat, however, is never the road to victory. You must come from that retreat with renewed determination to defeat the enemy of your marriage.

As the pastor in the introduction wisely understood, separation removes you from some of the constant pressure of conflict. It allows time for you to examine biblical principles for building a meaningful marriage. It permits self-examination in which emotions can be separated from behavior. It may stimulate a depth of openness in your communication that was not present before. In short, it places you in an arena where you can develop a new understanding of yourself and your spouse. Separation is not necessarily the beginning of the end. It may be only the beginning.

And if you are not separated but considering it, wondering

what future your relationship might have, you, too, are at the beginning of a long, challenging, yet potentially deeply rewarding journey. Or, as Gary Smalley has said, "Choose to receive this trial as an invitation to grow in humility and love."[3]

Let's get started.

GROWTH ASSIGNMENTS

1. Whether you are separated or in marital crisis, read the next chapter with an open mind. Examine your attitudes and actions.

2

how to start saving your marriage

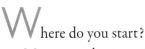

Where do you start?

Many couples in crisis sincerely want to save their marriages—but they feel pessimistic because the same issues, the same conversations come up over and over again. Some spouses wonder if it is possible to "save their marriage alone," to quote author Ed Wheat.[1] Others, as we have seen, are simply tired of the battle. It takes a tremendous amount of courage to overcome this skepticism and weariness and begin the work of healing. It takes courage to show kindness to someone who you feel has mistreated you, courage to speak the truth in love, courage to discard old habits of relating.

It also requires a realization that divorce is not the answer. Many years ago divorce was rare, something people in Hollywood did. Then from 1960 to 1980 there was a huge spike in the divorce rate,[2] and while it has flattened out to a degree, it is still too high—and too readily accepted as a solution. In fact, the very prevalence of divorce in our society makes it thinkable, just another option. When you see a sibling get divorced, or a friend or coworker, you might think, "Well, maybe . . ." But do not open that door!

The question, then, is: Are you willing to try? I want to begin this chapter by asking a very personal question, the same question I would ask if you were sitting in my office: Will you work on being reconciled to your spouse? Will you spend some energy, effort, and time finding out what can be done and then take constructive action?

I have already mentioned the walls spouses build between each other over time. Writer Judy Bodmer describes what happened in her young marriage:

> "I remember clearly the day I laid the first brick. We'd been married nine months. We went to a movie and I waited for Larry to reach over and take my hand, thus proving the magic was still there. But he didn't and as the movie progressed, I grew more hurt and angry. He shrugged it off, surprised I was upset over such a little thing . . ."
>
> Over time, she writes, the wall grew, "built with bricks of buried anger, unmet needs, silences, and cold shoulders. The marriage books we read made things worse; counseling confused the issues."

It got to the point where she began to think divorce might be the only answer—until she (wisely) realized she probably would end up marrying someone much like Larry. "And if I did, my problems would be multiplied by his kids, my kids, child support, and custody battles . . . God showed me I might escape my current pain, but in the long run, divorce extracted a high price. One I wasn't willing to pay."[3]

Judy knew she couldn't change her husband. But she could change herself. And that is what she set about doing, becoming more loving, more patient, less critical and demanding. It took a long time, but the result was the reward of a strong, deep relationship, "born out of suffering and obedience."

> Doing the hard work it takes to heal a marriage requires a profound sense that you do not wish to live without this person with whom you were once so joyfully united.

Doing the hard, sustained work it takes to heal a marriage is never easy. It may take time—Gary Smalley has said that the deeper the hurt, the longer the time to heal.[4] It takes honesty, courage, the willingness to repent, and a profound sense that you do not wish to live life without this person with whom you were once so joyfully united.

At the same time, there are constructive actions and positive behaviors a couple can take as they begin the reconciliation process. Particularly when a couple is separated, they can find themselves having the same *un*constructive conversations when they are together. But once a couple agrees to work on restoring their marriage, they are ready to solve the conflicts that drove them apart. Now they can work on the problem, not on each other. Let me offer several guideposts that will start to clear away some of those "bricks" so that you can begin the hard work of reconciliation.

"How Could You Do This to Me?"

James and Juanita have been separated for three months. He comes over once a week to visit Joy, their five-year-old. Sometimes he will take Joy out for dinner, and sometimes Juanita will invite him to eat with them. Most of the time James refuses her offer, but twice he has accepted. Juanita tries hard to be positive, but inevitably she finds herself accusing James of seeing someone else, and from that point the conversation degenerates.

Before long she is saying the now oft-repeated words, "How could you do this to me? How do you think it makes me feel? How do you think it makes Joy feel? Don't think she doesn't know what's going on! She may be young but she knows what you're doing."

James vacillates between retaliation and withdrawal when such attacks come. If he chooses to retaliate, he can be as verbal as she; but silence is his usual response, and he sometimes leaves while his wife is still sobbing. Juanita takes that as further rejection, and her hostility increases. Obviously, the road of separation is not leading them to reconciliation. If they continue that behavior they will be divorced.

Without realizing it, Juanita may be accomplishing exactly the opposite of what she wants. She has become a slave to her hostile emotions and negative attitudes. She makes their time together extremely unpleasant. What man in his right mind would ever want to come back to a woman behaving in such a manner? I am not saying he cannot return, for he can in spite of her behavior. (More on James later.) Juanita, however, is not working toward restoration, but toward a wider separation.

The first guidepost is: Guard your attitudes and actions; *keep them positive.* We cannot determine our emotions, but we can choose our attitudes and actions.

At the same time, acknowledge any negative emotions, but do not serve them. A better approach for Juanita would be to say, "James, you say you aren't seeing someone else, but I don't know what to think. I want to believe you but based on the past it's really hard. I do know that as long as you're having an affair we can never get back together. You will have to make that decision. In the meantime, I do not want to be controlled by my anger and I don't want to attack you during our times together and certainly not in front of our daughter."

Juanita is now emotionally free to be a constructive influence on James. She has admitted her feelings but is not controlled by them.

What about James? What are his feelings and thoughts? He may feel very unloved and may have angry, hostile feelings against Juanita based upon her past behavior. Those feelings also need to be acknowledged. His behavior may stem from an "I'll pay her back" attitude. He may reason, "She did not meet my needs for affection, so I was forced to turn elsewhere." Thus, he blames his wife for his behavior.

What will James do if he chooses to work on reconciliation? He might begin by identifying and acknowledging his own emotions. He might say to Juanita, "I have felt for a long time that you don't really love me. I've tried over and over but all I felt from you was cold . . . so I feel angry and cold toward you. But I hope that those feelings can be changed."

He must then be honest about the nature of his relationship with other women. If he has romantic feelings toward someone else, those must be discussed. Reconciliation must always begin where we are. Romantic feelings may be acknowledged, but not submitted to. Reconciliation will require breaking off any romantic affair that may exist. James might say to Juanita, "Yes, I am seeing someone. I'm lonely. This person makes me feel better. But I will break it off—if you are willing to help me restore our marriage."

If, on the other hand, James's relationships with other women are simply friendships without romantic feelings or behavior, then he must communicate that clearly. He might say, "Juanita, I can understand how you might find it hard to believe that there's nobody else. I'll do everything I can to show you there's no one else. I know the day will come when you can believe me again." With those attitudes and actions, James demonstrates his seriousness about his efforts at reconciliation.

The "Other Person"

Remember Allie and Zach at the beginning of this book? Allie discovered that after three years of marriage, Zach was seeing someone else, a woman he had met at a professional conference in the city. As soon as she discovered that, in her mind the marriage was over. She demanded Zach leave. He did.

Many separations have been precipitated because there was

someone else involved. The marital relationship has not been whole-some for many weeks. There is no warmth, understanding, or togetherness—remember, Allie had been feeling a distance from Zach for a while. In time, one partner meets someone else and falls in love or at least has a strong physical-emotional attraction that leads to an affair, whether sexual or emotional. At some point, the individual decides to separate, perhaps with the idea that somewhere down the road that new affair might lead to marriage.

> You do not like the idea of divorce, but an affair may seem much more meaningful than your marriage.

The husband or wife may or may not be aware of the other relationship. In some cases, the spouse will speak openly of the other person, and in others the spouse is extremely secretive. In either case, such activity is counterproductive to reconciliation. The second guidepost is: Avoid or abandon any romantic relationship with another adult. An affair should never be an option.

Do not misunderstand. I am deeply sympathetic with the dilemma an affair presents. You do not like the idea of divorce, but the affair may seem much more meaningful than your marriage. In just a few weeks or months perhaps you have come to love this person more than you love your mate. You are able to communicate with such freedom and understanding. It seems that you were meant for each other. How could it be wrong when it seems so right? You reason that God will forgive and in time everything will work out.

It is true that God will forgive if we genuinely confess and repent of our sin. Repentance, however, means to turn from sin. God will not forgive while we continue to sin. Nor does forgiveness remove all the results of sin. An incident in the life of David is a good example (2 Samuel 11:1–12:31). One morning while doing his exercises, he saw Bathsheba as she bathed herself on a rooftop. He liked what he saw, so he took steps to get a closer look. He brought her to the palace and eventually had sexual relations with her. Having sent her back home, he went about business as usual.

One small problem developed, however. Bathsheba sent word that she was pregnant. Her husband, Uriah, had been at war for months, so David ordered him home for rest and relaxation, hoping that he would make love with his wife and think the child was his. (Once we have sinned, we begin the process of covering up.) David's plan did not work because Uriah was more loyal to the military than David had imagined. He refused to go home to his wife while his brothers were in battle. David got him drunk, but Uriah's loyalty was stronger than the power of intoxication. Therefore, David moved to plan B.

He ordered Uriah to the front line, which assured his death. David was free to marry Bathsheba, which he did with haste. Now everything was fine, and they lived happily ever after. Right? Wrong! Read Psalm 51 if you want to hear the confession of a broken heart, written by a distraught King David.

We are never better for having sinned. Confession and forgiveness never remove the negative fallout of our wrong actions.

The emotional scars that come from separation and divorce are never removed. The hurt that is indelibly printed in the minds of children will never be erased. Our whole society has been deeply infected with the "throwaway neurosis." When you are no longer excited about it, get rid of it. It does not matter whether it is a car or a spouse. No wonder our children are so insecure. No wonder there is so little trust in marriage. One's word seems to hold no security.

I am sympathetic with the struggle and pain of losing the warm emotional feelings for one's mate and falling in love with someone else. But we cannot yield to our emotions. All of life is at stake. To follow one's emotions is the surest road to loneliness and ruin. More than half of those who marry new lovers will eventually divorce again.[5]

Our best interests are served by returning to our spouses, resolving our conflicts, learning to love, and rediscovering our dreams.

Divorce = Happiness?

The third guidepost is: Divorce will not lead to personal happiness. That truth was affirmed by the late Judith S. Wallerstein. An internationally recognized authority on the effects of divorce, Wallerstein began her research with the idea that while divorce may cause short-term pain, eventually splitting up will lead to long-term happiness. After extensive research with many families, she concluded that she was wrong. Divorce does not lead to greater happiness or more fulfillment for the couple or their children. In fact, the detrimental results of divorce follow the couple and the children for a lifetime. Her findings are chronicled in the classic study *Second Chances: Men, Women, and Children a Decade After Divorce.*[6]

I am not suggesting that the road to reconciliation is easy, but rather that it is right and that the results are worth the effort. Counselor and author Michelle Weiner-Davis says, "Over the last few years I have lost count of the many people I've worked with who were just about to give up on their spouses, but turned things around."[7]

You can too.

Feelings = Fail

But if you are violating Guidepost 2 and are entangled in an affair, let me suggest that you can break off the relationship with dignity, respect, and kindness to the other party. Breaking the relationship makes divorce less likely and reconciliation a distinct possibility. How does one break off an affair? First, indicate to the other person your concern for him or her. You need to confess your wrong in violating your marriage commitment. Firmly state your decision to work on reconciliation with your spouse. It is fine to share again your feelings for him or her, but affirm your choice to do what is right rather than what feels good. Remember, the surest road to failure in life is to follow your feelings. Your greatest happiness is in doing what is right, not in following your emotions.

What if you are the one left at home? Your spouse is having an affair and is now separated from you. Or, you may suspect he or she is having an affair and are contemplating separation. First, realize that the third person is never the full reason for separation. In fact, Guidepost 4 says that marital difficulty is caused by the marriage partners, not by someone outside the marriage. Therefore, each partner must work toward reconciliation. Almost always some failure in the marriage has developed over a period of time before an affair happens. Your failures and those of your spouse brought about the crisis in your marriage. Unresolved conflict, unmet needs, and stubborn selfishness eat away at a relationship over the weeks and months.

How shall you respond to your mate's affair? With displeasure, of course. But how will you express your displeasure? With angry outbursts of hate and condemnation? With depressions, withdrawal, and suicidal threats? By going out and having an affair yourself? You are disappointed, frustrated, and deeply hurt, but what will lead to reconciliation? None of the above. Yes, you need to express your feelings, but do not play servant to them. Tell your mate how deeply you are hurt, acknowledge your past failures, and ask for reconciliation.

Your spouse may not respond immediately, or the initial response may be hostile, but you have taken the first step. Second, refuse to let the affair be the issue, and resist the temptation to talk about it every time you get together. Concentrate on restoring your own relationship.

Your spouse may not break off the affair immediately, but the more you can do to resolve conflicts and communicate hope, the more attractive reconciliation becomes. When you are lashing out in anger or falling apart in self-pity, you do not make reconciliation very desirable.

Express hope and confidence that the two of you can find answers to your past failures. Your hope will tend to kindle hope in your spouse. Obviously you cannot be reconciled until your spouse breaks off the affair, but do not set time limits or demand any particular action. (Of course, if your separation also involved physical abuse or some other destructive behavior, you need to be very clear on what you expect of your spouse if there is to be any hope of reconciliation. We will discuss this further in chapter 7.) Allow time for your spouse to think, pray, and decide for himself or herself. You cannot force reconciliation—you can only make the prospects look bright.

It is important to add here that sometimes an individual may have emotional problems or issues from the past that contribute to the likelihood of adultery. Addictions, depression, and bipolar illness may be factors. Zach struggled with some very deep-seated, long-standing issues. A therapist can help you deal with these challenges.

Dating While Separated

If you are separated, you may be asking, "Should I date while I am separ-ated?" How many times have I heard that question? And, how many times have I given a hard answer? "If you are not free to marry, you are not free to date!" The fifth guidepost on the road to reconciliation is: Do not date during the separation period.

"If you are not free to marry, you are not free to date!" I first read that statement in Britton Wood's book *Single Adults Want to Be the Church, Too.*[8] After years of counseling the separated, I am more convinced than ever that Wood is right. When you start dating someone else while you are separated, you make reconciliation more difficult. The more you date, the muddier the water becomes.

I know that you have needs; you are lonely. Sometimes the load seems unbearable. I know that dating while separated is accepted, even encouraged, in our society. But most of those who are dating will never be reconciled. They will be divorced. Dating is a prelude to remarriage, not therapy for reconciliation.

Certainly you need friends. You need a listening ear. You need people who will care and help bear the load, but the dating context is not the best place to find such help. More about where that help can be found is in chapter 7.

You are extremely vulnerable during these days of separation. Unfortunately, there are those of the opposite sex who would like to take advantage of your vulnerability. Although pretending to be concerned about you, they are busy satisfying their own desires. I have seen many men and women devastated by such an experience. Your own emotions are erratic, and it would be easy for you to get infatuated with anyone who treats you with dignity, respect, and warmth.

Have you noticed the number of people who get married the day after they are divorced? Obviously they have been dating during separation. If the separation period is a time to seek reconciliation, why spend energy in an activity that leads to divorce and remarriage? Separation is not tantamount to divorce. We are still married while we are separated, and we ought to so live, whether or not our spouse complies.

I know this is difficult to accept, but I believe the present trend of open dating—including Internet dating—immediately after separation must be deterred. Such activity encourages and contributes to the divorce rate. If you believe in the power of human choice, then you must concede that your estranged spouse may well turn from his or her estrangement and seek reconciliation. You want to be prepared for that day if it comes. Dating someone else is not the way to be prepared. Develop friends, but refuse romantic involvement until the fate of your marriage is determined.

If you are not physically separated but your marriage is in crisis and you are wondering where to turn, you too may be vulnerable. Women in particular can be attracted to the coworker, husband of a friend, or small-group member who seems to "understand" them in a way their spouse does not. "Nothing is more inviting to a woman than the feeling that this person *gets* them, and when it seems he gets her in a way that old-shoe husband does not, watch out," noted one woman I know.

Again, I am sympathetic to your desire for warmth and companionship. But be aware of the risks.

What about Legal Arrangements?

"Shall we draw up separation papers, or does that make divorce more likely?" Many individuals feel that if they sign legal separation papers somehow that means that divorce is inevitable. Such is not the case. Many couples have experienced the joy of burning separation papers in celebration of reconciliation.

Separation papers, in states where they exist, are simply statements upon which both individuals agree that will guide certain aspects of their relationship while they are separated. The two biggest areas of concern are financial and parental. The questions are: How will we handle finances while separated? and What relationship will each of us have with the children?

The final guidepost, then, is: Move slowly in completing any legal separation papers. If a couple can take steps toward reconciliation within the first few weeks of separation, then separation papers are unnecessary. That is ideal. Why go to the expense of such legal work if you are going to get together and solve your problems? While you are physically apart, however, you need to mutually agree on some financial arrangement, and to discuss your relationship with your children if you are parents. If that cannot be agreed upon, it may indicate that one or both of you are not working at reconciliation.

> Love must not give license to an irresponsible spouse.

If after several weeks a couple is not moving toward reconciliation, then legal papers of separation may be in order. That is particularly true when the couple has been unable to reach an equitable financial arrangement and when children are being neglected or abused. In such cases, legal pressure may be necessary to force a spouse to be responsible.

Again, separation papers do not necessarily spell divorce, although in some states they are required before a divorce can be obtained. Separation papers do not determine divorce. What you do and say to each other during the separation period will determine that. Such papers can be destroyed at any point when the two of you are reconciled to life together instead of apart.

Separation is not the time for one spouse to walk on the other. And love must not give license to an irresponsible spouse. An individual who will not meet his or her responsibilities needs someone to hold him accountable. That may have caused part of the problem within the marriage. It must not be allowed to continue during separation. Legal pressure may be of help at this point. Legal papers do not mean that you cannot then be reconciled. If your spouse insists on signing legal papers, little is gained by resisting. You should simply make sure that you can live with the agreements you are signing.

Do not underestimate the matters we have discussed in this chapter. If you are going to work on reconciliation, it is essential that you choose a positive attitude, refuse to foster an extramarital affair, do not blame marital difficulty on someone outside the marriage, forgo dating, and treat each other with dignity and respect during the separation period. To violate those principles is to diminish the hope of reconciliation.

The growth assignments that conclude this chapter can help you to better understand yourself and take constructive steps toward reconciliation.

GROWTH ASSIGNMENTS

1. Which of your attitudes or actions will have to be changed
   if you are going to work on reconciliation?
   Make a list of five statements, each beginning "I will
   have to . . ."
2. Are you willing to make those changes? If so, why not start
   today? You need not announce to your spouse
   what you are doing—simply do it as you have opportunity.

3

change yourself, change your marriage

It has been said that unhappy marriages consist of unhappy people. As Judy Bodmer learned, you may not be able to change your spouse, but you *can* change yourself.

Marriages fail, we noted in chapter 1, for three primary reasons: lack of an intimate relationship with God, lack of an intimate relationship with your mate, or lack of an intimate understanding and acceptance of yourself. It is the last of those that we shall explore in this chapter. One might think we would begin with our relationship to God, but the fact is, one's relationship with God is greatly affected by one's self-understanding. This time should be used as an opportunity to rediscover your own assets and liabilities as a person and to take positive steps in personal growth. Even if you are not separated but are struggling with a marriage in crisis, it is possible—indeed, necessary—to look deeply at yourself and begin to make some changes.

Most of us tend to either underestimate or overestimate our value. We perceive ourselves as either useless failures or as God's gift to the world. Both of those extremes are incorrect. The truth is that your pattern of feeling, thinking, and behaving, which is your personality, has both strong and weak points.

"It Was Years before I Was Able to Accept Myself"

The person who feels inferior is emphasizing his weak points. If we focus on our failures, we appear to ourselves as failures. If we give attention to our weaknesses, we conceive of ourselves as weak. Inferiority often stems from a childhood in which parents or others have unintentionally communicated that we are dumb, stupid, ugly, clumsy, or not good enough in other ways.

A thirteen-year-old boy suffering from stomach ulcers once told me, "Dr. Chapman, I never do anything right."

"Why do you say that?" I asked.

"Well," he replied, "when I get a B on my report card my father always says, 'You should have made an A. Son, you're smarter than that.' When I'm playing baseball, if I get a double, my father says, 'You should have made a triple out of that. Can't you run?' When I mow the lawn, he says, 'You didn't get under the bushes.' I don't ever do anything right!"

That father had no idea what he was communicating to his son. His objective was to challenge his son to do his best, but in fact, he was communicating to the son that he was inferior.

Another woman admitted, "When I was growing up I felt like my sister was better than I was at so many things—that is, things that count when you're a kid. Like sports, being outgoing, having boys like you. She had straight hair when straight hair was really popular. I didn't. My parents never made me feel inferior—I did it to myself. It was years before I was able to accept myself, and I can still sometimes have flashes of those old feelings."

Usually feelings of inferiority are fed by constant comparison with others. The person who feels inferior will always compare himself with those who are better than he is. Of course, everyone can find someone more beautiful or handsome, more athletic, more intelligent. But what about the thousands who rank *below* you in those areas? The person who feels inferior will never choose to compare himself with those.

I am reminded of the spies' report as recorded in Numbers 13. Moses sent out twelve spies into the land of Canaan. The majority report (ten of the twelve) came back: "All the people we saw were huge. We even saw giants there . . . Next to them we felt like grasshoppers, and that's what they thought, too!" (32–33).

That "grasshopper mentality" is typical of those who feel inferior. Scores of women have said, "I feel so ugly, and I know that others think so too." One lady felt so ugly that she refused to go shopping because she did not want to be seen. Without exception those women were not ugly. They simply concluded that others perceived them in the same way that they perceived themselves.

Three perspectives go into any self-concept: (1) the way that I see myself, (2) the way that others see me, (3) the way that I think others see me. Numbers 1 and 3 are often identical, but number 2 is almost always different. People simply do not see us as we see ourselves. The person with inferiority feelings can be assured that 99 percent of the people who know him perceive him to be smarter, more attractive, and of greater value than he sees himself. Why live under the illusion that people think you are dumb, ugly, and useless when in fact that is not the way people perceive you?

"But Dr. Chapman," someone tells me, "you don't understand. People really do think I'm dumb." Then the person lists all the things that have happened since he was three years old that prove people think he is stupid. I can call in scores of people who can testify to the intelligence of the counselee, but that does not impress him. His mind is made up. He is dumb, and no one is going to convince him otherwise.

> One of the first steps in turning your thinking around is to realize that God has not given up on you.

No two people are alike. Therefore there are scores of people who have greater abilities than you in particular areas. In some tasks you excel. In others you have very little, if any, ability. That is true for all of us. Why should you exalt your weaknesses?

The Truth about You

Someone who struggles with low self-esteem may well blame themselves for the failure of the marriage. Then he or she will plead with the spouse for a chance to start over. When that is spurned, he or she may sink into deep depression and entertain thoughts of suicide. Those people allow the weakest part of their personalities (their feelings of inferiority) to control their behavior.

What is the answer to that downward spiral? One of the most powerful words in the Bible is the admonition of Psalm 15:2, which challenges us to speak the truth in our hearts. We are to tell ourselves the truth. Jesus said the truth liberates us (John 8:31–32).

Here are several truths about you. You are made in the image of God. You have tremendous value. Your abilities are many. You have scores of characteristics that others admire. Certainly you have experienced failure. Who hasn't? But that does not mean that you are a failure. You will be a failure only if you choose to fail. On the other hand, if you choose to succeed, nothing, including your feeling of inferiority, can keep you from your goal.

One of the first steps in turning your thinking around is to realize that God has not given up on you. The apostle Paul wrote, "For I am confident of this very thing, that He who began a good work in you will perfect it until the day of Christ Jesus" (Philippians 1:6 NASB). In spite of all that has happened, in spite of all your failures, God still intends to bring you to wholeness. He has some strong and positive purposes for your life. You must tell yourself the truth and behave accordingly.

"It's Their Fault"

The opposite personality type is the individual who feels that he or she is "the greatest." He can do no wrong. "If there's a problem in our marriage," he tells me, "it is obviously on the part of my mate." When confronted with his own failure, this narcissistic personality will admit in a philosophical way that he is not perfect, but insists that the real problem lies with his spouse.

This pattern of thinking, feeling, and behaving also begins in childhood. This is the "spoiled child." Very few responsibilities were enforced. The child grew up feeling that the world owed him a living. He became demanding of others. Impatient with others' imperfections, he often leaves a trail of broken relationships because he has taken advantage of people. He is very domineering and strong-willed. When he meets resistance from his mate, he attempts to force his spouse into line. When the spouse does not shape up, a person who feels superior may choose to separate, placing the blame on the spouse.

What truth will liberate the person with superiority feelings? It is an awareness that the ground is level at the foot of the cross of Christ. We all stand in need of forgiveness. When we feel superior at times, we need to recognize that we have failed as much as others have.

Perhaps you have been unwilling to admit your failures, although proclaiming loudly the failure of others. You are important, yes, but no more important than anyone else, including your spouse. You are intelligent, but intelligence is a gift of God for which you should be grateful. You have succeeded in reaching many of your goals. Great! Now learn to share the secret of your success with others and experience the meaning of Jesus' words, "It is more blessed to give than to receive" (Acts 20:35).

Have your feelings of superiority led you to conclude that you are superior? Then it is time for confession and repentance. Come down from your pedestal and enjoy life with the rest of your brothers and sisters. You do not have to claim perfection in order to be important. People will think no less of you if you admit your weaknesses. In fact, your spirit of superiority has driven people away from you in the past.

When a marriage is falling apart, and especially after separation, the typical narcissistic personality will blame his wife (or her husband) for the breakdown. Even if Mr. or Mrs. Superiority is the one who walked out or got involved in an affair, he or she will almost always blame the spouse for driving him to such action. If the spouse happens to have feelings of inferiority, he or she will probably accept the blame and suffer accordingly.

> The road to self-righteousness gets lonelier each day.

People with superiority feelings are quick to rationalize their sinful behavior. They know what the Bible says, but . . . they can give you a dozen reasons why in their case it is permissible.

The first step to recovery for the "I am superior" personality is to realize that you are human. No one is perfect. Locate your failures and admit them to God and to your spouse. Be as specific as you can. On the road to confession you will find many friends. The road to self-righteousness gets lonelier each day.

Can People Change?

We have looked at only one aspect of personality, that of inferior or superior attitudes toward oneself. Personality, however, covers the entire spectrum of human experience. When I use the word *personality*, I am speaking of your own unique pattern of thinking, feeling, and behaving. No two personalities are alike, although in certain aspects of personality people tend to fit into general categories. Most traits are expressed by contrasting words. We speak of an individual's being optimistic or pessimistic, negative or positive, critical or complimentary, extroverted or introverted, talkative or quiet, patient or impatient.

Our personalities greatly influence the way we live. The tragedy of our day is that we have been led to believe that our personalities are set in concrete by age five or six, and that our destinies are determined. Many feel trapped. They look at the thought, feeling, and behavior patterns that have caused them problems in the past and conclude that nothing can be done to change those patterns. But nothing could be further from the truth.

It is true that as adults those tendencies may persist. That is, we are influenced by certain personality patterns. Our lives, however, do not have to be governed by those patterns. The whole idea of education, spiritual conversion, and Christian growth stands in opposition to determinism, the idea that our quality of life is determined by patterns established in childhood. The message of the Bible is that we are responsible for the quality of the life we live. Our response to God, our conscious decisions, our choice of attitudes will determine that quality. We must not see ourselves enslaved by our personalities. We need to understand our personality patterns, to utilize our strengths for good, and to seek growth in the areas of weakness. Excel in your strengths and grow in your weaknesses.

What do you know about yourself? What kind of person

have you been through the years? Has your spirit been negative or positive toward life? One wife said, "My husband is so negative that when he wakes up in the morning he either says, 'Oh, no, I overslept!' or, 'Oh, no, I woke up too early!'" For that husband, every day started off wrong. With that attitude there is no way to win. That may appear foolish as you read it, but thousands of people choose to live life with just that attitude. Something is always wrong with everything. Could that be your attitude? If so, do you think it contributed to the breakdown of your marriage? Can you imagine the emotional drain on your spouse when he or she hears your daily newscast of doom?

Are you critical or complimentary toward others? Toward yourself? Look back over this day. Have you given yourself a compliment? Have you complimented anyone else? On the other hand, have you made a critical statement about someone? About yourself? Has that been a pattern of life for you? How has that affected your marriage?

What have been your patterns of communication? Do you tend to hold things inside or let them out? One wife reported, "My husband did not share with me what was going on in his life. He basically lived his life, and I lived mine. I did not like it, but I did not know what to do about it. One day he came home and told me he was leaving. I couldn't believe it. I had no idea that it was that bad."

How could such a situation arise? One or both partners yielded to a natural tendency to keep it all inside and slowly but surely put their marriage to sleep. Can such a marriage be healed? Yes, but it will likely require surgery (the skill of a counselor or pastor). Once our feelings are expressed, we can seek solutions.

No one, including your spouse, can work on a solution until he is aware of the problem.

Do you keep your feelings bottled up inside? Then use this time to learn to release those feelings. Find a counselor or trusted friend and ask for help. When you learn to communicate constructively with someone else, you can then communicate with your spouse. The tendency to keep quiet is not all bad. The Scriptures even challenge us to be "slow to speak" (James 1:19). It is when that tendency is carried to the extreme that it causes problems. As you discover your basic personality weaknesses, you will likely see how they have affected your marriage. Those patterns can be changed significantly with the help of God.

> Our history is not to be changed but accepted.

Accepting the Unchangeable

"Can an Ethiopian change the color of his skin? Can a leopard take away its spots?" (Jeremiah 13:23). Jesus asked, "Who of you by being worried can add a single hour to his life?" (Matthew 6:27 NASB). Those two questions have straightforward answers: of course not. Some things cannot be changed. Your height, skin color, bone structure, and color of eyes are pretty well settled unless modern medical science comes up with some new discoveries.

Perhaps the most influential unchangeable factor is your history. By definition, it cannot be changed. It is past. The past cannot be relived. Your parents, for better or worse, dead or alive, known or unknown, are your parents. That fact cannot be changed. Your childhood, pleasant or painful, is your childhood and stands as history.

Your marriage or marriages fall into the same category. It is futile to reason, "We should never have gotten married in the first place." The fact cannot be changed. The events that have transpired in your marriage are also history. You can undo none of them. No words can be retracted, no deed recalled. We can ask forgiveness for failures, but even that does not remove all of the effects of our sin.

Our history is not to be changed but accepted. When Jesus met the woman at the well, He did not ask that she erase her five marriages, for such would have been impossible; He simply offered her water that would quench her obvious thirst (John 4:5–29).

Do not look at the rest of your life as one great unknown.

We waste our time and energy when we ponder what might have been: "If only I had . . ." We must simply admit failure to ourselves, God, and our spouses. Accept God's forgiveness, forgive yourself, and trust that your spouse will do the same. Beyond that, you cannot deal with the past. You must concentrate on the future, for it is in your hands to shape.

Why not use this marital crisis to take an honest look at your personality? Discover your basic patterns of thought, feeling, and behavior. Then decide where your strengths lie and utilize them to expand your horizons. At the same time be realistic about your weaknesses. Decide what needs to be changed and take steps toward growth. Admit those things that cannot be changed and accept them. This could be a rewarding time of self-discovery and growth for you.

Something New, Something Good

Right now, of course, you may not have energy to make wholesale changes. You may have children to care for, work, the normal demands of life—plus the ongoing conflict and anxiety arising from a marriage in crisis. But I would encourage you if possible to take the time to do something for *you*. Read a novel or biography. Spend time in God's creation. Exercise more. Attend a concert with a friend. Take a gourmet cooking class.

I know that you may not feel like undertaking any of the above. Perhaps you have lost your interest in the midst of your loneliness and hurt. Sitting at home reflecting on your problems, however, will only lead to deeper depression. Once you take a step to develop an old interest, the sun may break through the darkness.

Concentrate on small, attainable goals at first. Do not look at the rest of your life as one great unknown. Make plans for today. What can you do today that will be constructive? As you fill your days with meaningful activity, hope for the future will grow.

Social media can be helpful, if you look for positive Christian content. Numerous websites offer help in self-understanding and biblical guidelines for marriage. (See page 155–56 for recommendations.) However, sharing your marital struggles on Facebook may elicit unwise advice from unqualified "counselors."

As you come to understand yourself, develop yourself, accept yourself, you enhance the prospects of reconciliation with your spouse.

GROWTH ASSIGNMENTS

1. Ask a pastor or counselor to arrange for you to take the Taylor-Johnson Temperament Analysis or the Myers-Briggs Personality Inventory. Either will help you identify personality patterns.

2. You may want to enroll in a class on personality development at your church or community college.

3. To get started in better understanding your personality, on a sheet of paper write answers to the following questions:

   - What do I like about myself?
   - What emotions do I feel today? Divide those into two columns:
     Negative feelings   Positive feelings
   - What do my negative feelings tell me about myself?
   - What do my positive feelings tell me about myself?
   - What are my emotional needs today?
   - How can I meet those needs in a responsible, Christian way?

- What would I like to see changed in my personality (i.e., my way of thinking, feeling, and behaving)?
- What step will I take today to effect that change?
- What do I dislike about myself but cannot change?
- Will I accept that characteristic and concentrate on my assets?

  Yes   No

4

turning to God

Our relationships with God may make or break our marriages. Augustine said, "Man was made by God and does not find rest until he finds God." If we look to a marriage partner to give us a sense of worth and to bring happiness, we are looking in the wrong direction. Many have expected a spouse to provide that which only God can give. Peace of mind, inner security, a confidence in the outcome of life, and a sense of joy about living do not come from marriage, but from an intimate relationship with God.

What has been your relationship with God during this time of marital crisis or separation? Many individuals find themselves angry with God—angry because God has allowed the pain, the loneliness, and the frustration that comes with a broken marital relationship. Others have found themselves turning to God in a fresh and deep way to seek God's help.

Read Psalm 77:1–15 (NASB), which follows. It is a personal expression of one individual who was going through a major crisis. You will note that there is first a description of the pain of being estranged from God and from others. But out of the midst of that pain, the psalmist turns to God and remembers more pleasant days when he knew the blessing of God and wholesome relationships with others in his life.

> My voice rises to God, and I will cry aloud;
> My voice rises to God, and He will hear me.
> In the day of my trouble I sought the Lord;
> In the night my hand was stretched out without weariness;
> My soul refused to be comforted.
> When I remember God, then I am disturbed;
> When I sigh, then my spirit grows faint.
> You have held my eyelids open;
> I am so troubled that I cannot speak.
> I have considered the days of old,
> The years of long ago.
> I will remember my song in the night;
> I will meditate with my heart,
> And my spirit ponders:
>
> Will the Lord reject forever?
> And will He never be favorable again?
> Has His lovingkindness ceased forever?
> Has His promise come to an end forever?
> Has God forgotten to be gracious,
> Or has He in anger withdrawn His compassion?
> Then I said, "It is my grief,
> That the right hand of the Most High has changed."
>
> I shall remember the deeds of the Lord;
> Surely I will remember Your wonders of old.
> I will meditate on all Your work

And muse on Your deeds.
Your way, O God, is holy;
What god is great like our God?
You are the God who works wonders;
You have made known Your strength among the peoples.
You have by Your power redeemed Your people,
The sons of Jacob and Joseph.

The passage ends with a very graphic description of King David's present state: "You have by Your power redeemed Your people." The word *redeem* means to "buy back" or "restore." That is always God's desire for His people. The process, however, may be painful. David wrote, "Your way was in the sea and Your paths in the mighty waters, and Your footprints may not be known" (v. 19).

As an adult separated from your spouse or struggling to save your marriage, you may feel that you are indeed walking through the sea in the midst of mighty waters and that you cannot see the footprints of God. But I assure you, God is vitally concerned about you and your present state. The words of Jesus, "Come to Me, all who are weary and heavy-laden, and I will give you rest" (Matthew 11:28 NASB), are directed to you as surely as they were directed to those to whom Jesus spoke.

Yes, you are weary from much stress. You are heavy-laden, burdened perhaps with guilt, anger, hostility, and anxiety. You will notice that Jesus does not ask that you lay the burden aside and come to Him, but rather that you just come. He has promised to give rest. He has not asked you to handle your own problems, nor has He promised to take away the problems, but He has promised rest.

God is your friend, if not your Father. The Scriptures teach He is the Father of all those who come to Him through Jesus Christ, His Son. He is not the Father of all—only of those who acknowledge Jesus Christ as Lord. But He is the friend of all. It is God's desire to share life with us, to help us find meaning and purpose in life, to give us answers to the problems we encounter. In the midst of our pain it is sometimes difficult to believe that God could do anything for us. May I suggest steps that will help you in personal spiritual growth during these difficult days?

Our Confession and God's Forgiveness

It may be true as you analyze your marriage that you discern your own role in that failure. On the other hand, it may be that you see more clearly the failures of your spouse, and you have spent many hours in accusing him or her of those failures. If Jesus' words in Matthew 7 were applied to marriage, they would read: "Why do you look at the speck that is in your mate's eye, but do not notice the log that is in your own eye? First pull the beam out of your own eye, then you can see more clearly how to get the speck out of your mate's eye" (see Matthew 7:3–5).

Our natural tendency is to seek to place blame with our mates and to reason in our hearts that if our mates would change, our marriages would be restored. Jesus said, however, that we must begin with our own sins. Whether that sin is large or small, it is the only sin that we can confess. If we confess our own failures, we will be better equipped to help with the failures of our spouses. When we fail our marriage partners, we also fail God, for Jesus admonished us to love one another (John 13:34). The only true way to express our love for God is by expressing our love for each other. When we fail to love each other, we have failed in our love for God. Therefore, we must confess the failures of the marriage to God.

> Forgiveness is God's promise that He will no longer hold our sin against us.

Perhaps the most powerful verse in the Bible on mental health is Acts 24:16, where Paul says about himself, "I always try to maintain a clear conscience before God and all people." Paul spoke from personal experience. He had learned that it takes discipline to deal with one's failure, but that discipline is necessary if we are to be emotionally, spiritually free. Thus, Paul said, "I empty my conscience toward God and toward men."

The process of emptying our conscience is confession. The word *confession* literally means "to agree with." Thus we agree with God about our failures. No longer are we excusing ourselves and our behavior, but we are acknowledging before God that we have sinned. The Scriptures teach believers that when we confess our sins, God "is faithful and just to forgive us our sins and to cleanse us from all unrighteousness" (1 John 1:9 ESV). The moment we are willing to acknowledge our failure, God is willing to forgive our sin. But as long as we excuse our sin, God will not hear our prayers (Psalm 66:18).

The first step, then, in developing your relationship with God is to confess all known sin. I suggest that you take pencil and paper and say to God, "Lord, where have I failed in my marriage?" As God brings truth to your mind, write it down and make a list of your failures. Then go over your list, confessing each sin, thanking God that Christ has paid the penalty for your sin, and accepting His forgiveness for that sin. The experience of forgiveness liberates us from the guilt that burdens us.

Confession and forgiveness do not mean that we will immediately lose all remorseful feelings about our sin. Forgiveness is God's promise that He will no longer hold our sin against us. We may still feel horrible when we reflect upon what we have done or failed to do, but our feelings have nothing to do with God's forgiveness. We must not allow those feelings to defeat us. When feelings of guilt return after confession, we simply say, "Thank You, Father, that those sins are forgiven and that You no longer hold them against me. Help me to forgive myself." Forgiving yourself is also a promise. You promise to no longer punish yourself for past failures. Such punishment produces nothing positive, but keeps you from making the most of your future.

When we confess our sin to God, it is as though we have come home from a long journey and our father welcomes us with extended arms, forgives our sin, kills the fatted calf, and makes a feast to celebrate our return (Luke 15:21–24). Such a return to God may be the most significant thing that happens while you are separated, for you are now returning to the One who made you and knows how to lead you in productive living.

"This Is Your Day in My Life"

Your relationship with God will grow only if you learn to communicate with Him. Remember, communication is a two-way process. Not only do we talk to God but God talks to us. Many people are familiar with prayer whereby we talk to God, but few people hear the voice of God. I am not suggesting that God speaks in an audible voice to us. But through the Bible, God speaks in a very personal way to those who will take the time to listen.

Some think of reading the Bible and praying as simply "religious" activities, but they are meant to be avenues of intimate fellowship between an individual and God. As we read the Bible, God will speak to us about Himself and about our lives. The Bible is more relevant than any book you will ever read on human relationships, for it is indeed the God of creation speaking to His creatures. Here are some practical ideas on communicating with God: since the Bible is God's Word to us, one ought to read it with a listening ear, an ear open to hear His voice. When we read other books, we are careful to underline the important ideas in each chapter. Why not do the same with the Bible? As you read the Scriptures, certain phrases, sentences, and ideas will stand out in each chapter. It is likely that those are the ideas God seeks to communicate to you. Why not underline, circle, or put a star by them to draw your attention to those ideas?

For many years I have followed the practice of daily sitting down with God, opening the Bible, and beginning the conversation with these words: "Father, this is Your day in my life. I want to hear Your voice. I need Your instructions. I want to know what You would say to me this day. As I read this chapter, bring to my mind the things You want me to hear." Then I read the chapter silently or aloud with pen in hand, marking those things that stand out as I read. Sometimes I read the chapter a second time, saying, "Lord, I'm not sure I understood what You were saying; I want to read this again. I want You to clarify what's on Your mind for me." I may underline additional lines or phrases.

Do not simply try in your own power to forgive, but ask the Spirit of God to enable you to forgive.

Having completed the chapter, I then go back and talk to God about what I've underlined, for if that is what God is saying to me, I want to respond to God. Many people simply read the Bible, close it, and then begin praying about something totally unrelated to what they have read. Nothing could be more discourteous. We would not treat a friend like that. If a friend asks a question, we give an answer. If a friend makes a statement, we have a response; so if God speaks to us through the Bible, we should respond to what God is saying.

For example, let us say that I am reading from Philippians, chapter 4, and the thing that impresses me is the statement in verse 4 (NASB): "Rejoice in the Lord always; again I will say, rejoice!" So I underline the sentence, and I circle the word *always*. Then I go back to God and say, "Lord, how can this be? It seems utterly impossible that I can rejoice always. Sometimes, yes, but always?" You see, I'm responding to what God has said to me with a question. I read the sentence again: "Rejoice in the Lord always; again I will say, rejoice!" and I see those little words in the Lord, and God has answered my question. What He is saying is that I am to rejoice in the Lord always, not in circumstances, for I cannot rejoice in adverse circumstances. But I can rejoice in the Lord in the midst of those circumstances. Because of my relationship with Him, I can indeed rejoice in the midst of my present problem. What an encouragement to one who is going through deep waters!

Every day God desires to speak to us in a very personal way from His Word, and He desires us to respond. May I challenge you to begin today by reading a chapter each day in the Bible, underlining and marking, then talking to God about what you have marked? Let me suggest that you begin with one book. (James is a good place to start.) Complete that book before beginning another. You will leave a trail through the Bible where you have walked with God, and you can easily refer back to the things God has said to you day by day and week by week. You will find that your relationship with God is greatly enhanced, for nothing builds relationships like open communication.

Choose to Obey

As you read the Scriptures, you will on occasion find clear commands of God such as "Be kind to each other, tenderhearted, forgiving one another, just as God through Christ has forgiven you" (Ephesians 4:32). Such commands are given for our good. God, who made us, knows precisely what will make us happy and fruitful in life. All of His commands are given with purpose, so we must choose in our own heart to obey every command we hear from God. Thus, if we read "be kind to each other," we ought to seek someone to whom we can be kind that day—someone to whom we can be tenderhearted, someone whom we need to forgive. Our example is Christ, who forgave us. You will remember that on the cross, Christ looked on those who were crucifying Him and said, "Father, forgive them, for they don't know what they are doing" (Luke 23:34). Is that not the attitude we should have toward those who wrong us? There are literally hundreds of commands in Scripture that will greatly enhance our lives as we respond in obedience.

We are not left to depend on our own power when it comes to obedience, for if we are Christians we have within us the Holy Spirit, who gives us the power to obey the commands of God. So if you find it difficult to forgive those who have sinned against you, there is help. Do not simply try in your own power to forgive, but ask the Spirit of God to enable you to forgive. Forgiveness is basically a promise. It is a promise that we will no longer hold a person's failures against him. It does not mean we are unaware of those failures, but it means we will not treat them as failures. It does not mean, in the strictest sense, that we will forget the sins, insofar as being aware they have been committed is concerned. But we are able, with God's help, to no longer hold the sin of another against him.

Can you envision what might happen in your life if you would begin reading the Scriptures daily, listening to the voice of God, and responding to His commands, in the power of the Holy Spirit? It is conceivable that in a few months you will hardly recognize yourself, for tremendous changes will take place day by day.

Sing to the Lord

Music is a universal expression of human feeling. If you listen to the songs of cultures around the world, you will find the themes of joy, excitement, and pleasure; but you will also find the themes of sorrow, pain, and hurt. That is true in both religious and secular music. Singing is a vehicle of communication. It can lift the heart or depress the spirit. The words of our songs determine whether they will lead us to depression or lead us to victory. Throughout the Psalms we are challenged to sing praise to the Lord. In the midst of pain, we may wonder, "For what can I praise God?" As we reflect upon the truth, however, we will find many things for which we can praise God.

In the psalm mentioned at the beginning of the chapter, David praised God for His past benefits, His past blessings. As we begin to praise God for what He has done in the past, we come to thank God that He will be faithful to us in the future. Paul wrote to the Ephesians that they were to be filled or controlled with the Holy Spirit, and then they were to sing "psalms and hymns and spiritual songs," making music in their hearts to the Lord (Ephesians 5:19).

Our songs of joy and triumph must grow out of our relationships with God. As we are controlled by the Spirit of God, we may sing of our problems, but the heart of our music will be praise to God for who He is and what He is doing in our lives.

Our relationships with God are not hindered by our present circumstances; instead, our circumstances may push us to God. You may not be inclined to sing. You may never have sung in your life, but as a Christian you can sing if only in private. In fact, Paul says we are to sing to ourselves. That may be in the shower, or it may be in bed. May I suggest if that is not a normal practice in your life that you simply take one of the psalms (remember, the psalms formed the hymnbook of the Jews) and make up your own tune and sing that psalm to God. Melody, pitch, and rhythm are unimportant. What is important is that you are expressing praise to God through the words of others who have walked through difficulty. You might begin with Psalm 77 (pp. 56–57).

Why Go to Church?

You may or may not currently be involved in a local church fellowship. During separation or when you're struggling in your marriage, it is particularly important that you find other Christians with whom you can fellowship. It is true that the church can be justly criticized. How often we hear individuals say, "I don't want to attend that church because it's filled with hypocrites." That is likely true. Hypocrites and sinners regularly attend most churches, but without hypocrites and sinners, who would be left to attend? For we have all sinned, and we are all sometimes hypocritical. Attending church does not mean we are perfect. It means that we are seeking growth.

In most Christian churches, you are likely to find friendly people who will welcome you and who will seek to help you. We were not meant to live alone. It was God who said in the beginning, "It is not good for the man to be alone" (Genesis 2:18). The psalmist also said, "God makes a home for the lonely" (Psalm 68:6 NASB). Right now you desperately need the fellowship of the larger family of God.

When many people think of church, they think only of attending the Sunday morning worship service. That is fine, but it is only a part of any church worthy of the name. The church is "the called-out ones," those who have responded to Jesus Christ as Lord and who come together to learn and to encourage each other. Small Bible study and prayer groups are vital in the fellowship of a church. Be sure that you do not just sample the Sunday sermon. Get involved in the small group studies where you can find answers to the questions that arise. Many churches offer classes designed to help the separated. Most pastors are also willing to give personal counseling.

If you have not been attending church regularly, start this Sunday. Find a group of Christians with whom you can identify and with whom you can come to share and who will give you the encouragement and support you need.

You must not come to the church with the idea of receiving only, but you must also come with the idea of giving of your ability to others. You may ask, "What do I have to offer anyone else? I can't handle my own problems." The fact is, you will probably encounter others at the church who have problems similar to yours, and you may be able to share with them something you are discovering in your relationship with God. Attending church is never a one-way street. We are told in Hebrews 10 that we are to exhort, comfort, and encourage each other, and that is likely to take place in any Christian church that is authentic.

It is important to add here that if you find that a pastor or church leaders are not responsive to your marital concerns, then you may need to try to find another church. Churches vary widely in their ministry to hurting marriages.

Pain, Joy, and Sharing Life with God

Earlier I mentioned the words of Jesus, inviting all who are weary and heavy-laden to come to Him (Matthew 11:28). Jesus went on to say, "Take My yoke upon you, and learn from Me, for I am gentle and humble in heart, and you will find rest for your souls. For My yoke is easy and My burden is light" (11:29–30 NASB). Jesus does not call us to lay down our load in order to find rest. He calls us to take His yoke upon us. The yoke speaks of work. We are challenged not to inactivity, not to simple rest, but we are challenged to take upon ourselves the yoke of Christ and to blend our lives with the lives of other Christians in accomplishing good for God in the world.

Jesus says, "My yoke is easy and My burden is light." Compared to what? Compared to the yoke and load we bear when we choose to walk our own way. As we walk our own way, giving no thought to God or His Word, we find our yoke is heavy and our load becomes heavier as the days come and go. But as we walk with Christ we find His yoke is easy, His burden is light compared to what we have borne before. And His burden is always with purpose. Yes, there is work to be done, but that work is purposeful.

I have known many separated individuals who have spent hours of dedicated service helping the church office or janitorial staff or in reaching out to those who are sick or in trouble. Your own pain does not render you ineffective with others. Indeed, it may equip you to share with others. The road to happiness is not found in isolation, concentrating on one's problems; the road to happiness is found by sharing life with God and learning to serve Him.

GROWTH ASSIGNMENTS

If you have not already done so, ask God to bring to your mind the areas in which you have failed in your marriage.

1. Make a list of your failures and confess each one to God. Thank Him that Christ has paid the penalty for those sins, and accept His forgiveness.
2. Begin the practice of reading, marking, and talking to God about a chapter in the Bible each day. You may want to begin with the book of James in the New Testament.
3. Try singing a psalm to God. Make your own tune and rhythm. You may begin with Psalm 1.
4. If you are not active in a local church, decide today which church you will visit next Sunday. Be sure to attend the Bible study class as well as the worship service.
5. Don't give up the search until you find a warm, loving group of Christians with whom you can share life.

5

love is . . .

If you are separated, your spouse is no longer coming home at the end of the day. When you walk into your home, no one is there to greet you. If you love at all, it must be at a distance and sporadically expressed. Some separated couples have a great deal of contact, whereas others see each other seldom, if ever. Thus, some of you will have more opportunity than others to express love to your spouses. Do not decry your circumstance. Your situation is your situation, and you must make the most of it. Using the descriptive words of 1 Corinthians 13, I want to suggest some practical ways of expressing love while separated. If you are not separated—yet—but going through a marital crisis, Paul's words may also be of much help to you as you struggle to communicate courteously and constructively.

Patience

"Love is patient" (v. 4). Don't get in a hurry. Your marriage did not fall apart overnight, and it will not be rebuilt today. Don't set time limits for yourself or your spouse. We operate best when we are free. If you are separated, you want him or her to come of his own volition. Give him time. Express your desire, but step back and let him decide.

Be patient also with your spouse's ambivalence. During a marital crisis or separation, individuals are emotionally pulled in two directions. Some desire, however faint, for the fulfillment of earlier dreams pushes one toward reconciliation. On the other hand, there is the pain and hurt of a sick marriage that emotionally pushes him or her away. As we've already seen, there may also be someone else to whom he is attracted, thus the emotional pull in that direction. A person may sincerely say one thing today and something else tomorrow. He is not intending to lie. He is simply reporting his feelings at the moment. It is to be hoped that he or she will learn not to make decisions based upon feelings but upon what is right. In the meantime, however, you must be patient with his contradictory statements. The expression of understanding is even more helpful: "I understand that you are pulled in two directions. I feel that myself sometimes."

Kindness

And love is "kind" (v. 4). The word that is here translated "kind" means "to be useful or beneficial." Thus, kindness may be words or actions that are useful or beneficial to the other person. What can you say or do that will be useful or beneficial to your spouse? If you are a husband who has left, there are scores of things around the house you could do for your wife if she is willing. If your wife has left you, you may still be able to do some "useful or beneficial" things to make her life more pleasant. Don't hold back simply because she walked out on you or has drifted from you. If she will allow, you can be God's agent of love toward her. What is to be gained by not helping her? If you don't, someone else will, and you will have missed an opportunity to express love by being kind.

"Love builds up" (1 Corinthians 8:1 ESV). How can you "build up" your spouse? One way to edify your spouse is to express kindness in your speech. Say something that is useful or beneficial—something that will build up rather than tear down. Much of our normal conversation while separated or in marital crisis is destructive. We express our hostile feelings with cutting words that emphasize the failures of our spouses. Reconciliation is paved with words of kindness. You are both having a struggle with self-image. You both feel badly about what happened. You both feel guilty because of your own failures. Why not build up your spouse by complimenting him on some of the good you see in him?

We can also build one another up by what we do not say— that is, by listening. Addressing men, Gary Smalley urges husbands to listen "to her perceived pain instead of arguing or being defensive." He cites Proverbs 11:12 (NIV): "A man of understanding holds his tongue."[1]

Some time ago, I read the story of a woman who went to a marriage counselor and confided that she wanted to divorce her husband. "I want to hurt him in the worst possible way," she said. "What do you suggest?"

The counselor replied, "Start showering him with compliments. When he thinks you love him devotedly, then start the divorce action. That's the way to hurt him most."

She returned in two months to report that she had followed his advice.

"Good," said the counselor. "Now is the time to file for divorce."

Undeserved love is the highest form of love and the most powerful thing you can do for someone who has wronged you.

"Divorce!" cried the woman. "Never! I've fallen in love with the guy!"

What had happened? She had started expressing love to him by using compliments. In time, he began to feel loved and began to express love to her.

Yes, warm emotions can be reborn. But kind words and acts must *precede* warm emotions. Many couples feel that a trial separation will help them get their feelings straightened out. They want to separate and have no contact to see if time apart will cause the warm feelings to return. Such a process is futile. Attitude and action must precede positive emotions. Distance alone will not turn emotions around.

I know it may seem impossible to be kind to a spouse who has inflicted so much pain. It may take time and the help of a pastor or counselor to work through your hurt. You may be asking, "Can I ever be kind when they have been so unkind to me?"

The answer is yes. Jesus is our model and He can give us power to love the unlovely. Undeserved love is the highest form of love and the most powerful thing you can do for someone who has wronged you.

The Envy Game

Love "does not envy" (1 Corinthians 13:4 NIV). Each spouse usually thinks the other has the best end of the bargain while separated. The wife with children will complain that her husband is free to do what he pleases, whereas she must stay at home with the children. The husband complains that with all the money she demands, he can't afford to live, let alone enjoy life.

The envy game leads a wife to have an affair because her husband does. It leads the husband to skip town, forsaking his responsibility for children, to get away and find happiness. The truth is that separation is rough on both of you. Neither of you has an ideal situation. There are added pressures on both. Finances, logistics, loneliness, meaning to life, all cry for answers. You are living in an abnormal state. Husband and wife were not made to live separated. They were made to live in family unity. Emotionally, physically, spiritually, and socially your best interests are served in seeking to reconcile your differences and finding marital unity. Don't envy your mate's position, but pray and work toward the union of two halves now separated and hurting.

I have heard people who were separated or struggling in their marriages say they felt "sorry" for their spouses. What about the role of compassion? Empathy?

Humility

Love "is not . . . boastful or proud" (v. 4). It is so easy to look back and announce all of your righteous acts in the marriage while overlooking your weaknesses. "I was faithful to you. I listened to your problems, took care of things around the house, worked hard every day, was there for you . . . and where did it get me? I did everything I could. What about me? I– I– I–." Such talk is true, but it is not loving.

Your past record speaks for itself. You do not need to toot your own horn. Your friends know you. Your children know you. You know the truth about yourself. God knows you totally. And your spouse knows you, though they may choose to accentuate the negative at the present time. Love will refuse to proclaim its own goodness. Remain humble, and trust God.

Courtesy

Love "is not . . . rude" (v. 4–5). The opposite of rudeness is courtesy. You do not have to treat each other rudely simply because you are separated. The word *courtesy* means "court-like in manners." Treat your spouse with dignity and respect as if you were courting. He is estranged, and you are seeking to win his affection. Can you remember how you treated him before marriage? If it was respectful, then return to those actions and words.

There is no reason for arguing and screaming when you are together. "A gentle answer deflects anger, but harsh words make tempers flare" (Proverbs 15:1). Certainly you need to discuss issues, but you do not need to attack each other in the process. I know we sometimes get angry, but we are instructed not to sin in our anger (Ephesians 4:26). For practical suggestions on how to communicate constructively in the midst of conflict, see the section on communication in my book *The Marriage You've Always Wanted*. (See resources.)

If your mate is open to the idea, why not step back from your problems from time to time and just spend time together, doing things you both enjoy? Don't feel that you must always hash out your differences. While together, treat each other with courtesy. Do those little things that you know the other appreciates. Speak with kindness. Put the other's interests first. Rediscover each other's assets. Like Ann and Steve, the couple who drifted apart because they were being pulled in different directions through various circumstances, you may find that the very act of spending focused time together begins to pull you back together. Counselor Michelle Weiner-Davis notes that it is important to begin by focusing on a couple's strengths and building from there. [2] Start with the positive!

Unselfishness

Love "does not demand its own way" (1 Corinthians 13:5). When most of us got married, we were thinking of what we would get out of the marriage. We had dreams of our own happiness and of what our mates would do for us. Certainly we wanted them to be happy also, but our chief thoughts were on what marriage would mean to us.

After the wedding we found that our mates did not always think of our happiness. They did not always meet our needs. More and more they demanded our time, energy, and resources for their own happiness. We felt cheated and used. So we fought for our rights. We demanded that our spouses do certain things for us, or we gave up and sought happiness elsewhere.

Happiness is a unique commodity. It is never found by the person shopping for it. You may search the shelves of the whole world for personal happiness and never find it at any price. Lonely men and women in every age have grumbled and complained at the futility of their search for happiness. Genuine happiness is the by-product of making someone else happy.

What can you do for the happiness of your spouse? Admittedly, this is a difficult question. "But I don't care if he's happy," you say honestly. "What about me? I want to be happy for a change!"

Your feelings are understandable—but how will you find happiness? You must discover the needs of someone else and seek to meet those needs. Why not begin with your spouse?

"It's really, really important to observe your spouse, understand their reactions."

Of course, finding out what those needs are can take some insight, because your spouse may not be able to tell you directly. Jane, married for more than thirty years, shares a valuable lesson. "It's really, really important to observe your spouse, understand their reactions. My husband gets angry when he feels bad about himself. Last Christmas he was wrangling the Christmas tree into its stand, and it kept falling over. I was upstairs, working in our home office, and he came up all grouchy. At first I didn't understand and said, 'But this should be *fun!*' and then I realized that he wasn't crabby with me, but with himself. Men don't much like to admit inadequacy, especially when it comes to something like that.

"So his need at that time was for me to truly *hear* him and respond accordingly. I also had to put aside what I was doing and put him first."

Forgetting the Past

Love "keeps no record of being wronged" (v. 5). How many times in a counseling session have I listened as a husband or wife spent hours detailing the past words and actions of his or her spouse? Some can go back and replay the minute details of events that happened fifteen years ago. Each time they replay the event, they relive the emotions of the moment.

The hurt, pain, and disappointment are all felt as though it happened yesterday. I ask you, of what value is that? It is fine to share it once with a counselor, but to replay it daily in your own mind is worse than useless. It is destructive.

All of us have failures in our closets that could be pulled out by our mates and used to destroy us. Yes, we are guilty of horrible failures, but the great message of the Bible is that there is forgiveness. Christ died for our sins, so that we might be free from condemnation. "There is therefore now no condemnation for those who are in Christ Jesus" (Romans 8:1 ESV). Forgiveness means that God no longer holds our sins against us. He never reminds us of past failures.

We need to follow God's example in the treatment of our spouses. Yes, we have been wronged, but we have the power to forgive. If your mate confesses and asks forgiveness, you must never again bring up the past. No positive purpose is served by bringing up specifics again and again. Your well-being is not determined by the past, but by what you do with the future. What is important is how you treat each other today, not how you treated each other last month. Forgetting the past is the key that can open the future, bringing reconciliation between your spouse and you.

Trust

Love "always trusts" (1 Corinthians 13:7 NIV). "Can I ever trust him again?" a wife asks. "How can I learn to trust her after what has happened?" asks a sincere husband. Trust is an essential ingredient to marital unity. When we trust our mates, we believe in their basic integrity. We feel that what they say is true. We have no reason to doubt. When an individual violates our confidence and is not truthful, however, trust is fractured. When that happens more than once, trust diminishes and in time disintegrates.

Can trust be reborn? Yes, if integrity is reborn. Trust dies when integrity dies. If we will confess our sins and ask forgiveness, we are forgiven by God. It is to be hoped that our mates will also forgive us. At that moment the seed of integrity is planted again. It takes time, however, for trust to come to fruition. Trust was not destroyed overnight, and it will not flourish immediately. Yes, we can come to trust again, but such trust will be built upon a record of integrity. It takes time to establish such a record. We must water the tender plant of integrity until its roots sink deeply into our relationships again.

Without hope, all will fail.

On a practical level this means that if your trust in your spouse is to be restored, your spouse must establish a new record of trustworthiness. Your mate must do what they say they will love is . . .

do. The person must be honest in all of his or her dealings with you. Without trustworthy actions, trust cannot grow. Every time you find your spouse telling the truth, your confidence in them will grow. Trust can be restored during this crisis, but only if your spouse begins a new pattern of being trustworthy.

If you are the offender, then you will enhance the rebuilding of trust on the part of your spouse by inviting him or her to investigate your behavior. Every time your mate discovers your actions matching your words, trust grows. It takes time, but you can become a person of integrity and your spouse can come again to trust you.

Hope

Love "is always hopeful" (v. 7). I think the greatest thing a counselor brings to the counseling room is hope. A listening ear, a caring heart, communication skills, biblical teachings—all are necessary to successful counseling, but without hope, all will fail. That spirit of hope was born out of difficulties resolved in my own marriage and encouraged by the hundreds of couples whom I have seen find wholeness. It is rooted in the powerful teachings of the Bible.

In the early years of our marriage, Karolyn and I despaired of hope. It seemed that our dream would not come true. We loved each other (we thought), but we could not resolve persistent conflicts. We held to our own ideas of what the other should be and do, but neither of us lived up to those expectations. I knew the pain of seeing the one thing I wanted most in life, a happy marriage, seemingly slipping away with each passing day.

We did not physically leave each other, but we were separated emotionally.

There was no simple solution, no magic wand that changed our lives, but we stayed with each other until attitudes changed. Books, conferences, friends, and God all worked together to help us see that much of our destructive behavior grew out of our own insecurities. We came to understand ourselves better, particularly the assets and liabilities of our own personalities. We started listening instead of talking. Asking instead of demanding. Seeking to understand rather than seeking to get our own ways. We came to appreciate each other's strengths and to help each other in the weak areas. We came to see ourselves as friends. The warmth and security of our moments together now are a long way from the pain and hurt of those earlier years, but I remember, and I have hope for others.

The gospel of Christ is the "power of God at work, saving everyone who believes" (Romans 1:16). Through the years I have seen lives changed radically whenever men and women have committed themselves to Christ. The simple message of the gospel is that not only will God forgive our sins through our faith in what Christ did on the cross, but that the Spirit of Christ will actually come to live in us and give us power to change. All men and women have the power to change, but the Christian has the specific help of the Holy Spirit when he or she chooses to walk God's way.

Yes, there is hope for you and hope for your marriage. The first step is to turn your life over to God, and the second step is to love your spouse in spite of all that has happened. Certainly there is a real possibility that your mate will not respond to your love or to the love of God. But God will not leave you without hope.

You have a future with God. That future involves every effort toward reconciliation. God will direct your steps in fruitful living. Your ultimate fulfillment is not dependent upon the response of your mate, but upon your own response to God.

GROWTH ASSIGNMENTS

1. In an attitude of prayer, think and then prepare a list of specific ways you could express God's love to your spouse.
2. Make another list of the things you must stop doing or saying if you are to be God's agent of love toward your spouse.
3. Pray that God will enable you to cease all destructive words and actions toward your spouse.
4. Select one of the actions you listed under number 1 above and ask God for an opportunity to express His love to your spouse this week.
5. Commit yourself to walk with God regardless of what your spouse does.

6

tough love

By now, you may be saying, "But, Dr. Chapman, what about me? I can't talk to my spouse or be kind to him. I have had to take the children and move out for my own safety." Or I think of Tim, whom we met in the beginning of this book. Tim is the victim of repeated verbal abuse. What do we say to Tim?

Let me make it clear: *Some things are not permissible in a marriage.* When physical abuse, sexual unfaithfulness, sexual abuse of children, alcoholism, or drug addiction persist in a marriage, it is time to take loving action. In fact, one is not loving when they accept such behavior as a way of life. Love is always concerned about the well-being of the other person. It is not loving to accept this behavior and do nothing. Such behavior is destroying the individual and the marriage. Love must confront. That's tough love. And that's real love.

Confronting—and Redeeming

In the Bible, confronting is always seen as redemptive. "If your brother sins against you, go and tell him his fault, between you and him alone," Jesus says in Matthew 18:15 (ESV). "If he listens to you, you have gained your brother"—

won him over. The hope of confronting is that the relationship might be restored.

We know, however, that repentance is not always the response of the offender. Jesus goes on to say, "But if he does not listen, take one or two others along with you, that every charge may be established by the evidence of two or three witnesses. If he refuses to listen to them, tell it to the church. And if he refuses to listen even to the church, let him be to you as a Gentile and a tax collector"—that is, a pagan (Matthew 18:16–17). How do you treat a pagan? You pray for him. You reach out to witness to him of God's grace, but you do not accept his sinful behavior. Upon repentance, you are fully ready to forgive and restore. In fact, that is the desired outcome of confronting.

So first, we go to the individual privately. We share not only our displeasure with the person's behavior, but we affirm that such behavior is sinful. It violates the laws God established for marriage and family. We urge the person to return to God and to turn from his or her destructive behavior. We assure the spouse that we love him or her too much to sit idly by. We cannot condone such behavior. If the spouse repents, we forgive and continue to grow in the marriage.

If the individual refuses to deal with the sinful behavior, we share the situation with two or three others, and they go with us to confront him or her again. These should be trusted, mature people who understand how to be kind but firm. Perhaps the knowledge that others are aware of the situation will motivate the spouse to reach out for help in breaking destructive patterns. If they are willing to go for counseling, then the process should be started as soon as possible. And it should continue as long as necessary until the counselor and both the husband and wife agree that the problem has been dealt with in a comprehensive manner. With individual counseling and the support of a caring Christian family, destructive patterns can be changed. Marriages can be restored.

The third level of confrontation is to share it with the church. When the spouse does not see the need to repent after you have confronted your spouse and two or three others also have, then the church becomes involved. Usually this begins by telling a pastor or staff member as a representative of the church. The pastoral leader takes a representative group from the church and again confronts the erring spouse. Perhaps now he or she will respond positively to the help that is being offered and the process of healing can begin.

While this may seem too much to ask, and some pastors may not be willing to get involved, it is clearly the biblical pattern. In my experience, it is often the visit of the pastor or elders that God uses to touch the heart of the spouse and begin the process of reconciliation.

If there is still no willingness to deal with the problem, we are told to treat the individual, in a sense, as a non-Christian. If we apply this principle to the marriage relationship, does this mean separation? In my opinion, that would certainly be one alternative. The purpose is still redemptive. The separation is for the purpose of creating a crisis that we hope will urge the spouse to take constructive action. We pray for them, love them, and stand ready to receive them when they turn from their destructive behavior.

Separation as an Act of Love

Some Christians see separation as always a sinful action. In reality, it may sometimes be the most loving action one can take. Let me illustrate.

Joyce was waiting outside the lecture hall where I was to speak. As I approached, I could tell that she had her eye on me. "You're Dr. Chapman, aren't you?" she asked. No need to pose as Gary Smalley at that point, so I confessed. She continued, "I've been waiting for you because I have a question about your lecture last night. Your talk on love was very painful for me. I've been separated from my husband for three months. I have a question I want to ask. Is there ever a time to stop loving?"

"Why do you ask?" I replied.

"My husband physically and emotionally abused me for eight years. He refused to work. I supported the family for seven years. Then I got sick. Even then he refused to get a job."

"Was he able to work?" I inquired.

"As able as I was. He was working when we married. Six months later, he lost his job and would never take the initiative to look for another. I was working, so he stayed home with the children and watched TV. Mainly he watched TV. He still expected me to do all the cooking. Even when the youngest child started school, he still wouldn't look for a job.

"I just got tired of it. I gave and gave with nothing in return. I got to the place where I had no more love to give. Was I wrong to stop loving him?"

"Maybe you didn't stop loving him," I said. "Maybe you are loving him more now than before. As I understand the biblical concept of love, it is looking out for another person's interests. It is putting their well-being above your own."

She interrupted, "That's what I did for all those years, Dr. Chapman, but I couldn't do it any longer."

"I understand that was your intention all those years," I said, "but I'm not sure your behavior was all that loving. In reality, you helped him live an irresponsible lifestyle. Did you really help him? Was it really beneficial to him? You made it possible for him to live without working, whereas the Bible says that 'if a man will not work, he shall not eat' [2 Thessalonians 3:10 NIV]. Your actions helped him violate that basic biblical principle."

I could tell this was not the way Joyce expected this conversation to go. I continued, "Now in separating you have taken a step to help him follow this principle. You have said, 'I will no longer encourage you to disobey the Bible. I can't make you work, but I will not help you shirk responsibility.' Who knows, he may get a job."

"Oh, he has already promised that he will get a job and will be kind to me if I will come back," she said.

"Then let's see if he follows through on his promise. Let him get a job and let him go with you to see a pastor or a counselor to discuss the abuse problems. In time, perhaps you can have a healthy, biblical marriage. But let him know that you will not come back until these things are dealt with thoroughly. You must have some evidence that things can be different. Do you understand why I would say that you may be loving him more effectively now than before? Don't misunderstand me. I am not encouraging divorce. I am saying that love uses confrontation as a means of trying to help.

Some Christians define love as totally placating the mate's desires without regard to his or her behavior. This is something that God Himself does not do.

"Love says to a husband, 'I love you too much to help you do wrong. I will not sit here and let you destroy yourself and me by cursing me every night. I cannot make you stop cursing, but I will not be here to receive it tonight. If you want to make our lives better, then I am open. But I won't be a part of letting you destroy me.'

"Your attitude is not to be one of abandonment but of love," I continued. "To answer your original question, there is never a time to stop loving someone, but there is a time to start expressing that love in a different, more effective manner. Love is not letting someone step on you. Love is caring so much for their well-being that you refuse to play into their sick behavior. Many people are healed when someone loves them enough to stand up to their inappropriate actions."

God's Tough Love

God is our best model in this kind of boundary-setting love. Over and over again, we read passages similar to the following words to Israel:

If you pay attention to these laws and are careful to follow them, then the Lord your God will keep his covenant of love with you, as he swore to your ancestors. He will love you and bless you and increase your numbers. He will bless the fruit of your womb, the crops of your land—your grain, new wine and olive oil—the calves of your herds and the lambs of your flocks in the land he swore to your ancestors to give you. (Deuteronomy 7:12–13 NIV)

If you ever forget the Lord your God and follow other gods and worship and bow down to them, I testify against you today that you will surely be destroyed. (Deuteronomy 8:19 NIV)

Such boundary setting has been interpreted by some as non-Christian and unloving. In reality, it is love at its best. Without boundaries, all of life becomes confusing. "Good fences make good neighbors," poet Robert Frost wrote.[1] That's not just good poetry; it's good sense. Some things are not permitted in a marriage. Love is willing to draw a line and refuse to accept the behavior as normal. Such tough love may not lead to reconciliation, but it is a responsible and loving action.

Some Christians define love as totally placating the mate's desires without regard to his or her behavior. This is something that God Himself does not do. It is true that God loves us unconditionally, but it is not true that His approach is the same whether we obey or disobey His commands. He has established boundaries, and when we are true to these boundaries, we experience "blessing." When we violate or rebel, He loves too much to be silent.

Sometimes in the name of love or out of fear, we put up

with destructive behavior in a spouse until we come to hate the person. Then we take action out of self-defense. How much healthier to take action earlier in the relationship while we still have emotional energy with which to endure the process. "Putting up" with sinful behavior is never God's way. He loves too deeply for that.

The earlier we can clarify boundaries and respond when they are violated, the better. We cannot have the benefits of a warm, loving relationship unless we are willing to be responsible for our own behavior.

What about Abuse?

Perhaps you have separated—or are seriously considering it—due to physical or verbal abuse, sexual unfaithfulness, sexual abuse of children, alcohol or drug abuse—or some other behavior expressly condemned in Scripture. If so, let me encourage you to work closely with a pastor or Christian counselor in determining where you should go from here. Your act of separating may have been a conscious act of tough love or it may have been simply an act of self-preservation. Whatever the case, you would profit from the perspective of a professional who has had experience in helping spouses respond to such abusive situations.

You will face many questions during your separation. If there has been a pattern of physical abuse or sexual abuse of children, do you allow the spouse you have left to come back into the house for a visit? In my opinion, not until there has been considerable counseling and the counselor agrees that such a visit would be safe. A promise to change is not enough in these cases. Promises have been made before. Real change in established patterns of abuse is not likely to occur without extensive counseling and the help of the Holy Spirit. Remember, our goal is reconciliation, not simply getting back together. Getting back together without dealing with real problems is almost certain disaster.

Tough love may seem to be harsh, but it is sometimes necessary. Firmness with kindness is the proper approach. We cannot be reconciled with an abusive spouse until the abuse has been dealt with thoroughly. We must be open to walk the long road of healing, but we dare not ignore the abuse. Ignored abuse only escalates. Better to set the firm boundary of tough love now than later. Later may be too late!

GROWTH ASSIGNMENTS

1. Which of the following were part of your spouse's behavior in your marriage? (Put his or her initials by the ones that apply.)

   ___ physical abuse   ___ verbal abuse

   ___ sexual abuse of children   ___ sexual unfaithfulness

   ___ alcohol abuse   ___ drug abuse

   ___ other _____

2. Which of the above were part of your own behavior in your marriage? (Put your initials by the ones that apply.)
3. What steps have you taken to deal with your own destructive behavior?
4. What steps has your spouse taken to deal with their destructive behavior?

5. If any of the above are established patterns in either of your lives, there can be authentic reconciliation only after these behavior patterns have been changed. Almost always, this will require the help of a pastor or professional counselor. If you are not yet seeing a pastor or counselor, you may want to take steps immediately to find such a person and make an appointment.

   Also, make sure that your spouse understands that there can be no reconciliation without counseling. Tell them that promises of change are not enough. If your spouse is serious, he or she will be willing to seek help.

6. If your spouse is not willing to go for counseling about these destructive behavior patterns, then you may want to secure your own counselor so you will have help in knowing how to set tough-love boundaries with your spouse.

7

loneliness: "the deepest pit"

Several years ago, I spoke to our congregation about the role of single adults in the family of God. In describing some of the problems faced by singles, I mentioned the pain of loneliness. The following week, I was approached by a young mother, separated from her husband, who said, "I don't think you know what you're talking about." I was taken aback for a moment. "What do you mean?" I asked.

"Your sermon last week about loneliness—I don't think you have any idea what it means to be lonely. You have a wife who loves you. How could you know what it is like to be lonely?"

I acknowledged that she was quite right. "I'm certain that I do not know the pain you are going through," I admitted. There is a sense in which no one knows the pain that another experiences. We can only listen to those who hurt, and try to understand.

I reflected on the words I had written some months before when I was away from my family for three weeks while teaching a course on single-adult ministries at a West Coast college: "It has been a long time since I have felt the loneliness I have experienced this afternoon and evening. Three thousand miles from home and friends gives one a feeling of emptiness. Hundreds of people are on campus, but I know none of them. The students seem to know one another and feel at home. I feel very alone."

The pain I felt that night, the isolation of being unknown by any of the people around me, was nothing compared with the aloneness that young mother felt. I knew that in time I would be coming home to a loving wife and caring children. I envisioned that reunion. I lived with that dream. But that young lady had no such vision, no such dream.

"Being lonely in a marriage is way more difficult than being lonely as a single person."

A young man said to his pastor, "I've had two lonely years. I don't mean lonesome; I mean lonely. Do you know the difference between lonesome and lonely? No! You have never had to, because lonesome is when somebody is not there and you know they will be back after a while. Being lonely is when you don't have anybody to be lonesome for.

"I was lonesome for a long time after they left. But that was when I thought they were coming back. I'm not blaming them. I'm not saying it wasn't my fault. Most of it was. But they are not ever coming back. Not in a million years. You don't know what hell is! And I hope you never do!"

Counselor Samuel Rainey observes, "Being lonely in a marriage is way more difficult than being lonely as a single person.

The hopes and expectations that come with a lifelong commitment will become unbearable at some point when [those] needs are left unmet."[1]

Lonely—and Heartsick

Whether we are physically separated or living under the same roof but emotionally estranged from each other, loneliness is real! What many do not realize is that it can be deadly. James J. Lynch, professor of psychology and scientific director of the psychosomatic clinic at the University of Maryland School of Medicine, has made an extensive study of the relationship between loneliness and physical health. In an interview, Dr. Lynch was asked how close the connection is between loneliness and health. He responded: "That's like asking what is the connection between air and one's health. Like the air we breathe, human companionship is taken for granted until we are deprived of it. The fact is that social isolation, sudden loss of love, and chronic loneliness are significant contributors to illness and premature death. Loneliness is not only pushing our culture to the breaking point, it is pushing our physical health to the breaking point."[2]

Researchers Jack H. Medalie and Uri Goldbourt studied 10,000 married men age forty years or older to determine factors contributing to angina pectoris, a type of heart disease. The study, conducted in Israel, followed the men during a five-year period. The study revealed that fewer of those who had loving and supportive wives developed heart disease than did those whose wives were "colder" (52 per 1,000 versus 93 per 1,000).[3] An intimate relationship in marriage enhances physical health. Loneliness within the marital relationship is detrimental to health.

Loneliness for the separated, however, seems to be even more acute. One woman, writing in the *Christian Medical Society Journal*, vividly described the pain: "Loneliness is perhaps the deepest pit which blocks the path of the separated. After several years of marriage, I missed not having anyone with whom to share the little events of each day. Mealtimes were especially lonely, and cooking for one seemed pointless. Mothers have children to cook for and talk to, but nonetheless, they long for adult companionship. Not having children myself, I plunged into activities so that I wouldn't have time to reflect on how empty my life was. At church or at a party I often felt isolated, especially if no one made an effort to sit with me."[4]

Robert S. Weiss, professor of sociology at the University of Massachusetts, who has pioneered in the exploration of loneliness, identifies two forms of loneliness—emotional and social.[5] Although the symptoms differ, the cause of both types of loneliness remains the same: the inability to satisfy the need to form meaningful attachments.

Emotional loneliness springs from the need for intimacy with a spouse or a best friend. A person who is emotionally lonely feels that there is no one he can absolutely count on. Symptoms include feelings of tension, vigilance against possible threat, restlessness, loss of appetite, an inability to fall asleep, and a pervasive low-level anxiety.

In social loneliness the individual experiences a sense of detachment from the community at large. He experiences the feeling that "what matters is taking place elsewhere."[6] Often the divisions of the day become meaningless to the socially lonely. They may doze in the middle of the day and awake in the middle of the night. Social loneliness is especially pronounced among individuals who have no significant vocation. They sense that their lives are not accomplishing anything worthwhile.

The separated are likely to experience both kinds of loneliness. That is especially true when one does not have a social support system outside the marriage. The wife who has been at home through the years will likely feel cut off not only from her husband but also from the whole world when separation occurs.

Loneliness is sometimes mistaken for depression. Though lonely people may eventually become depressed out of frustration at their inability to dispel loneliness, the two are very different states: depression resists change; loneliness produces pressure to change. Depression renders one immobile, whereas loneliness will press one to move in any direction that offers hope. That is why many lonely people move toward singles bars, feeling all the while that they should not go. Depression keeps one at home with all the shades drawn in self-pity.

What Are You Doing with Your Life?

Social loneliness, that feeling of being cut off from all that is significant in the world, may be cured when you become involved in a meaningful vocation. Much of our sense of worth comes from what we are doing with our lives. If I feel that my life is making a genuine, positive contribution to God and the world, I am not likely to be troubled with social loneliness. I am not cut off but have become an active, meaningful part of what is significant in my generation.

For some, that may mean going back to school to prepare for the vocational dream that has been dormant many years. I

am reminded of one wife in her middle thirties who upon separation enrolled in the local technical institute, finished her high
school work, developed administrative skills, and now feels very
much a part of her vocational community. The sense of belong-
ing to a team that is making a significant contribution to the
world brings emotional healing from social loneliness.

Such training may also build your self-confidence. As
you demonstrate that you can be successful in the classroom,
you feel better about yourself, and you stretch your vision
of what God may have for you in the future. You doubtless
have many undeveloped interests and abilities. This may be
the best possible time to begin their cultivation.

Such vocational and personal development may well serve
as a stepping-stone to reconciliation
to your spouse. As he or she sees
you seizing the opportunity for
growth rather than succumb-
ing to the paralysis of suffering, he is more likely to
see hope for a more mature
marriage. Your mate can
see you becoming a different and better person. Such
constructive change brings a
breath of fresh hope. On the other
hand, your positive action does not
guarantee his or her return. What it does guarantee is the healing of social loneliness.

Some mothers will feel such vocational training is impos-

> You spend more
> time with yourself
> than anyone else.
> Why not make the
> time pleasant?

sible or undesirable. They feel limited or fenced in by the children. Let me remind you that children are a gift of God (Psalm 127:3). They are no less a blessing when you experience separation. You will be spared much of the loneliness that others experience because of your relationship with your children. In terms of significant vocation, none is more rewarding than training children. Many other vocations involve working with "things," but you are dealing with persons. Your commodity is eternal; theirs is temporal. It is still true that "the hand that rocks the cradle rules the world." Do not decry your situation if you cannot work outside the home. Thank God for your opportunity and make the most of the greatest.

On the other hand, some mothers who do not desire to work outside the home are forced to do so by the separation. The husband cannot or will not provide adequate financial support, and the wife is pressured to work. If you feel such pressure, view it as an opportunity rather than an oppression. Ask God to give added physical and emotional strength. Ask for the wisdom of Solomon in training your children and move out to be God's woman. Social loneliness will not be one of your problems.

For those who cannot work or go to school, there are many opportunities for involvement in meaningful projects in your community. Civic groups are always looking for volunteers who are willing to invest time and energy. Christian groups such as Christian women's clubs and Christian businessmen's committees will help channel your abilities into meaningful activities. You need not stay on the sidelines—you can be on the team! You can have the sense of accomplishment that comes from a wise investment of your life.

Leaving the Cocoon

The ultimate answer to emotional loneliness, the lack of an intimate relationship with another person, is to reach out and establish wholesome contact with yourself, God, and others. We have discussed all of those in previous chapters, but let me say again that you have the capacity to be your own best friend. You spend more time with yourself than anyone else. Why not make the time pleasant? Learn to like yourself and create an atmosphere in which you can enjoy life. You need not destroy yourself because of what has happened. You have admitted your failures—now get up and do something today that will make you feel pleased with yourself.

The church can greatly assist you in making meaningful contact with God and others. It is a joy to observe what happens when a lonely, separated person enters the life of our church. In the sermon he hears hope, which he has not heard for many weeks. In the informal study groups he meets people who are finding that hope for themselves. He discovers people who are not perfect, but forgiven, who reach out to him in love. Week by week, little by little, a person comes to respond to God and to those hands of hope. He learns to talk to God and to hear His word for him. He learns to share himself with others who genuinely care. In time the loneliness fades, and the beauty of that once dejected individual begins to unfold like a fragrant rose. Few things are more rewarding for those of us who minister in the fellowship of a local church.

Does it sound too easy? Too "religious"? I assure you, it is neither easy nor otherworldly. In the first place there is a great deal of risk on your part. You must move out from the bondage of your cocoon. Yes, you can learn to fly, but the cocoon must go. You can learn freedom from loneliness, but you must leave your room in search of a caring fellowship.

Unfortunately, you will not find the warmth you need in all churches. Some groups have become a mutual aid society for those who pay their dues, rather than a lighthouse for battered ships. But don't give up. Jesus said, "Ask, and it will be given to you; seek, and you will find; knock, and it will be opened to you" (Matthew 7:7 ESV). Your searching will not be in vain.

> It is desperately tragic when hurting people come to our services and leave without a healing touch.

One warning as you go. Seek Christian love, not marriage. Remember, your goal is reconciliation with your spouse. You want to keep all roads open in that direction. In the meantime, you need the love and care of others. Again, don't expect perfection in those whom you meet at church. You may even find individuals in the church who will try to exploit you. The church does not stand at the door to check the character of all who attend its activities. As Jesus said, the wheat and the weeds grow together until the time of harvest (Matthew 13:24–30).

Of all the social institutions of our nation, no organization is better equipped to care for the needs of the lonely than the church. The church offers not only a social support system, but a spiritual support system as well. To be rightly related to God and warmly related to His creatures is the best medication available for loneliness.

Let me digress a moment and say a word to church members. We must accept the challenge of creating the kind of fellowship I have described above. It is desperately tragic when hurting people come to our services and leave without a healing touch. As one older woman put it, "I sit in the pew next to a warm body, but I draw no heat. I am in the same faith, but draw no act of love. I sing the same hymns with those next to me, but I hear only my own voice. When it is finished, I leave, as I came in, hungry for a touch of someone, someone to tell me I am a person worth something to them. Just a smile would do it perhaps, some gesture or sign that I am not a stranger."[7]

As Paul Tournier wrote,

It is the church alone, nevertheless, which can answer the world of today's tremendous thirst for community. Christ sent His disciples two by two. The great body of the early Christians, according to the Bible, "were of one heart and soul; they had all things in common" (Acts 4:32; 2:44). Instead of demonstrating the way to fellowship to the world today, the church seems to embody the triumph of individualism. The faithful sit side by side without even knowing each other; the elders gather in a little parliament with its parties and formalities; the pastors do their work without reference to one another.[8]

May we never be satisfied until the churches with whom we minister see themselves carrying on the ministry of our Lord who said, "Come to Me, all who are weary and heavy-laden, and I will give you rest" (Matthew 11:28 NASB).

Whether you meet people at church, in your community, or at the grocery store, you must take the initiative in reaching out to others. Emotional loneliness will not go away simply with the passing of time. You need the fellowship of others, and you must take the initiative in establishing relationships.

Others may not come to you, but as you express interest in others by initiating conversation, they will become interested in you. When you show concern for the well-being of others, you will find that concern being returned to you. As you build caring relationships, emotional loneliness dissipates.

Let me say a word about social media. While it is certainly a place to meet people, it is not the safest place. And while you may communicate with friends and family on social media, it is face-to-face relationships that are safest and most helpful.

The title of James Johnson's thoughtful book pungently proclaims the truth: loneliness is not forever. You may feel locked into a hopeless situation. You are separated, but not divorced. Free to hurt, but not to remarry. Lonely and alone. But just as separation is a temporary state, so loneliness is only a passageway—a hallway, not a living room. On one end of the hall is depression, immobility, pain, and darkness, but on the other is life, love, and meaning. You are in the middle of the hallway. Perhaps you are even lying on the floor crying. But eventually, you will get up.

When you do, I hope you will start walking (perhaps crawling at first) toward the door of hope. Just through that door are some loving people who will accept you as you are and help you become what you want to be. Loneliness is not forever!

GROWTH ASSIGNMENTS

1. Clarify your feelings of social loneliness by answering the following:
   - Do you feel cut off, removed from all that is worthwhile in the world?
   - Do you see others accomplishing meaningful goals while you sit in the stands and watch?
   - If you could do anything in the world with your life, what would you like to do?
   - Is that goal realistic for you? If not, what would be a realistic goal?
   - If you were to accomplish that goal, what would be the first step?
   - How will that step affect your relationship with your spouse?
   - What will such a step do for you?
   - Why not take that step and ask God to steer you into what is best?
2. Clarify your feelings of emotional loneliness by answering the following:
   - Do you feel emotionally alone? That there is no one with whom you can share your honest feelings?
   - What opportunity and freedom do you have to share your feelings with your spouse?
   - Is there a friend with whom you can share without fear of being rejected? If so, have you shared your

present pain with that new friend? Why not do so today?

- Do you feel the need to develop friendships with others? Where, in your community, could you go to develop such friendships?
- Are you presently involved in a Christian fellowship? If not, what keeps you from doing so immediately?

3. If loneliness is acute, and you have been unable to share with anyone, make an appointment with a counselor or pastor, who can help you see your situation more objectively.

8

"i'm so angry"

I am so angry when I think of him. When I think of all that he has done to me, I literally hate him. I get furious when I think about it. I know it's not right, but I can't help it." The anger of this separated woman is almost palpable.

"When I saw the guy she was dating," recalls a man in the process of divorce, "I'll have to be honest: my first thought was to kill both of them."

"Before my friend got divorced, she despised her husband so much she could not look at him, and he couldn't look at her. They didn't talk. No relationship. They were just too angry," said a young woman.

When we come to the point of marital crisis or separation, usually one or both spouses have lost their love feelings. We have been hurt. We have been wronged. Our spouses are responsible, and our hostile feelings are directed toward them. We want to strike back at them and make them suffer as we have.

Usually both individuals feel some anger, since each views the other as responsible for his pain. Though anger is normal, it is also destructive. Anger may destroy its object, but more often it destroys the one who harbors it. If anger can be expressed in a wholesome, constructive manner, it can lead to desired change, but if left to smolder within, it can be devastating. Unexpressed anger produces death, like a malignant cancer slowly destroying life's fiber.

Uncontrolled expression of anger is like an explosion that destroys everything in its range. To rant and rave, scream and shout, jump and kick serves no constructive purpose. Such an outburst is like an emotional heart attack and may produce permanent damage—including to children.

> Anger may appear on center stage for a brief moment, but it must not be allowed to interrupt the drama of your life.

Many of us are familiar with Paul's words, "Be angry, and yet do not sin; do not let the sun go down on your anger, and do not give the devil an opportunity" (Ephesians 4:26–27 NASB). But note Paul did not say, "Don't get angry!" That would be unrealistic. All of us experience feelings of anger when we think we have been mistreated. Rather, Paul says, "In your anger, do not sin!" Don't be so controlled by your feelings of anger that you do or say something destructive and thus sinful. The implication is that we are to be responsible for our actions *even when* we are angry.

Anger makes one very prone to sinful behavior. If we simply do what comes naturally, we will lash out against the person or object of our anger. Most murders in a domestic situation occur in an atmosphere of anger or drunkenness, and sometimes both. Tensions escalate, and tragedy results.

I have heard husbands who physically abused their wives, weeping and repeating, "I didn't mean to do it. I didn't mean to do it." Wives and husbands who verbally abuse each other often say afterward, "I regret the things I said. I wish I could recall my words. I did not mean what I said."

The Right Kind of Anger

So how can we be responsible for our actions, even when we're angry? The challenge is to *refuse to be controlled by your feelings of anger.* Confess your anger to yourself, God, a friend, or a counselor, and to your spouse, but don't be controlled by it. When you talk about your feelings with someone else, you dissipate the anger and are far more likely to do something constructive.

Paul also warns us not to let anger stay with us as a permanent guest. It may appear on center stage for a brief moment, but it must not be allowed to interrupt the drama of your life.

So the best way to get rid of anger is to confess it. The worst thing you can do is to repress it. When you hold it in and tell yourself that you are not angry, you are setting the stage for a volcanic eruption of gigantic proportions.

You are also infecting your soul with bitterness, which is nothing more than repressed anger. It is anger held in so long that it becomes a fixed way of thinking and feeling. You become locked into constant thoughts of how you might hurt your spouse. You replay past failures over and over again. Each time you feel the hurt, the pain, the anger as though it just happened. Again and again you ask the same questions and get the same answers. You hear the tape play until it crowds out everything else in your mind. Anger has descended into bitterness, and you are now filled with the malignancy of hate. You say that your spouse has made your life miserable, but in reality you have chosen the company of anger. No one can embrace anger without becoming infected with bitterness and hatred.

If your anger has turned into bitterness, you will likely need the assistance of a counselor or pastor to help you extract the infection and lead you to the healing waters of God's forgiveness. Yes, you have a right to feel angry, but you do not have the right to destroy one of God's creatures—yourself. The feeling of anger cannot be avoided, but bitterness results from daily choosing to let anger live in your heart. Thus we read, "Get rid of all bitterness, rage and anger, brawling and slander, along with every form of malice" (Ephesians 4:31 NIV). We must confess bitterness as sin and accept God's forgiveness.

We should note that a one-time confession of bitterness may not alleviate all hostile feelings. If the bitterness has been there a long time, the feelings that accompany the bitter attitude may die slowly. What do you do when thoughts and feelings of anger and bitterness return? Acknowledge those thoughts and feelings to God and affirm your commitment to forgive. An appropriate prayer might be: "Father, You know my thoughts and feelings, but I thank You that with Your help, I will no longer focus on the failures of my spouse. Now help me as I move out to be an agent of Your love." You must refuse to harbor resentment. As you practice love, the angry, bitter thoughts and feelings will occur less and less.

Once freed from bitterness, we are challenged to "be kind to each another, tender-hearted, forgiving one another, just as

God through Christ has forgiven you. Imitate God, therefore, in everything you do" (Ephesians 4:32–5:1). We must not stop with acknowledging our bitterness and accepting God's forgiveness. We must also release our anger and our spouses to God and ask Him to fill us with love instead of hate. God is not only concerned that we be freed from anger, but that we be agents of love and kindness as we discussed earlier.

That is the marvelous message of the Bible. God does not want us to be enslaved to any negative emotion. Rather, He wants us to have a love relationship with Him that will spill over into our relationships with others. Anger focuses on an area of conflict in our relationship. We are to seek to resolve that conflict. If our spouses will not help us deal with that conflict, we must refuse to be victims of anger. We may allow anger entrance into our lives, but we cannot allow it to take up residence.

The Danger of Retaliation

Uncontrolled bitterness has a way of fostering revenge. When we yield to the "get even" spirit, we are violating the clear teaching of Scripture. Paul says, "Never pay back evil with more evil . . . never take revenge. Leave that to the righteous anger of God" (Romans 12:17, 19). You may have been greatly wronged by your spouse, but it is not your responsibility to punish him for his sin. He must face God with his sin, and God is a just judge.

Again Paul says to the Thessalonian Christians, "See that no one pays back evil for evil, but always try to do good to each other and to all people" (1 Thessalonians 5:15). The emphasis is upon seeking what is good for your spouse, not upon getting even. Seeking his good is not the same as overlooking his sin. As we have already discussed, it is not good to allow your spouse to continue an irresponsible, sinful lifestyle. You are to seek his or her good, not with angry threats, but with carefully considered admonitions.

Anger and bitterness are often expressed in destructive verbal explosions. But verbal retaliation accomplishes no constructive purpose. Far better to confess that we are angry and therefore cannot discuss the issue positively and prefer to wait until we can handle our feelings. Issues need to be discussed; conflicts need to be resolved; but we will find no solution in the heat of anger.

Don't condemn yourself for feeling angry. That feeling indicates that you are a member of the human race. You have the capacity to become deeply moved about something you think important. Great! Let that concern lead you to constructive action. Don't become enslaved to your anger and do something that will make the situation worse. Acknowledge your feelings of anger to God and a friend and ask both to help you respond creatively and redemptively to the situation.

GROWTH ASSIGNMENTS

1. Express your anger in writing. Ask God to guide you as you try to express your feelings. You may begin, "I am angry because . . ."

2. Think of a friend who will be objective, with whom you may share what you have written. Ask him or her to listen

as you read and then to help you find constructive ways to deal with the issue.

3. Do you feel that you have allowed your anger to develop into bitterness? If so, are you willing to confess it as sin and accept God's forgiveness?

4. If you have never invited Christ into your life, as you confess your sin, why not invite Him to come into your life and give you power to deal with your present problems?

5. For additional help in processing anger, see Gary Chapman, *Anger: Handling a Powerful Emotion in a Healthy Way* (Chicago: Northfield, 2006).

9

rebuilding

Sometimes an individual says to his spouse, "I want you to be happy. If leaving will make you happy, then leave. It hurts, but I want you to be happy." On the surface that may sound very loving and self-sacrificing, but in reality it is neither. Love seeks the good of the spouse.

It may seem easier to separate and pursue your own happiness than to work at reconciling differences and rediscovering love. It may be much harder to stay together than to separate, especially when feelings of love have gone. The Christian's call is not to the easy road, but to the right road. I can promise you that the right road leads to both happiness and love after the pain of reconciliation.

The choice to return to your spouse and pursue reconciliation is a step of faith. But it is not blind faith. It is faith based upon the counsel of God. You cannot see the warmth of emotional love returning. You cannot see differences resolved. You cannot see the intimacy that you desire from a marriage. You must take the first steps, therefore, by faith, not by sight. With your hand in God's hand, you must walk with Him, trusting His wisdom. What you see will be only through the eyes of faith.

Reconciliation demands a choice. It is a choice against

continued separation and ultimate divorce. It is a choice to reaffirm your marital vows and actively seek to discover the intimacy and fulfillment God had in mind when He instituted marriage. It is not a choice to go back to the kind of relationship you had when you separated, but to work toward establishing something far more meaningful.

The choice for reconciliation is not popular in our day. A thousand voices will seek to lure you to the supposed happiness of life "free" from your spouse. Others will call you to join them in sex without commitment. You stand at the crossroads. The decision is yours.

To paraphrase the poet Robert Frost, reconciliation is definitely the road "less traveled by,"[1] but it too will make all the difference.

The Road Back

Let us assume that you have made your choice in favor of reconciliation—or committing together to give your marriage another try. Let me walk with you down that road "less traveled by." First, before you take another step, why not tell God about your decision? Yes, He knows your heart and thus your decision, but God is a person, and He likes to hear your voice. It may seem awkward to pray aloud if you are not accustomed to such conversation, but go ahead. Tell Him how you feel, where you have been, what you have done. Confess your failures and ask for forgiveness. Tell Him of your decision to seek reconciliation with your spouse, and ask for His help. (Remember, He will not force your spouse to reciprocate, but He will enable you to be loving in your attempts.) Ask Him to change you into the person He wants you to be. Ask for guidance as you walk the road to reconciliation.

With the assurance of God's forgiveness and God's help you will now want to invite your spouse to join you in the hard work of rebuilding your marriage. Perhaps you could invite your spouse for dinner or suggest you go out together. If he or she is reluctant, tell him that you have something very important you would like to discuss with him. If he cannot have dinner with you now, suggest that perhaps the two of you can get together in a week or so. Do not pressure your spouse. Spend the week praying that God will prod, encourage, and motivate him to respond.

Be patient; be persistent. Your persistence and patience will eventually indicate your seriousness. When you eventually express your decision to seek reconciliation, he or she will likely take it more seriously. It may be that God will use the intervening time to prepare him for what you have to say.

During or after the dinner, tell your spouse that you have been doing a lot of thinking and praying about your marriage. Indicate that you are coming to understand yourself more fully and that much of your behavior has been controlled by your emotions and attitudes. Tell him you have come to realize that you do not have to be a slave to your feelings and that attitudes can be changed. Admit that you have failed in many ways, and ask forgiveness for those failures.

Tell your spouse that you have been reading a book that has stimulated your thinking and has helped you come to the decision that you want to work on restoring your marriage. You may say, "I know that I will not be able to do this without your help.

I understand if you feel reluctant. I know that there is not much in the past that would encourage you to try again. But I do not want us to try as we have tried in the past. I want us to work at something far more meaningful than we have ever had. I want us to take whatever steps are necessary to gain self-understanding and understanding of each other. I know that it will take work, and may be painful, but I am willing to do whatever is necessary."

> Your objective is not to "get back together." Your objective is to give rebirth to your marriage.

Indicate that you do not expect an answer right away. You want him or her to think and pray about it. You may want to give him a copy of this book and suggest that he read it. Tell him that in reading the book he will perhaps understand some of the things you have been thinking and your decision to seek reconciliation. Suggest that after your spouse has had sufficient time to think, read, and pray that he or she agree to discuss things further.

Don't expect all problems to melt after such an evening. You have only taken the first step on the road "less traveled by." Where do you go from here?

When Both Are Willing

In chapter 10 we will discuss what you must do if your spouse is not willing to work toward reconciliation. In this chapter, let us assume that your spouse responds affirmatively. He or she is as willing as you are to work at restoring the dream you had when you were married. Should you move back into the same apartment or house immediately? Probably not. Remember, your objective is not to "get back together." The objective is to give rebirth to your marriage. The conflicts, frustrations, misunderstandings, and unmet needs that led you to this crisis point must be examined and resolved.

For most couples, the process of restoration will require the services of a pastor or marriage counselor. You need to develop skills in expressing your feelings in a constructive way. You must come to understand and appreciate the thoughts and feelings of your spouse. You must find ways to meet each other's emotional and physical needs. Marriage counselors and many pastors are trained in helping you develop such skills.

If you are attending a church, why not call your pastor and tell him of your decision to seek reconciliation and ask if he would have time to help you learn how to relate to each other creatively, or if he could recommend someone who could. Not all ministers are skilled in marriage counseling, but most will be able to direct you to help if they cannot help you. As you meet with the pastor or counselor and develop your communication skills, you will begin to feel freedom in your relationship. You will begin to feel more understanding. You will begin to reach agreement on issues that have been unresolved conflicts. You will give each other the freedom to disagree on certain issues and yet be kind and loving to each other.

For those who have been physically separated, as you begin to see such growth taking place, you will want to discuss and decide when you should move back into the same apartment or house. There is no precise rule; some couples will be ready to move back together after three or four sessions with the counselor or pastor. For others, it will be after twelve or more sessions. Don't stop seeing the counselor when you move back together. That is an important time. It will bring some added pressures, and you will need to concentrate on open, loving communication during those days. Continue with your counseling until you feel you have adequately dealt with unresolved conflict and developed skills in handling disagreements. The communication skills you learn will be important for the rest of your life. You must not neglect them when the crisis is over.

Some couples will not be able to secure the services of a trained counselor. Fortunately, other sources of help are available. There is a wealth of excellent books, Internet resources, podcasts, and conferences within reach of almost any couple today. My book *The Marriage You've Always Wanted* (Moody Publishers) was written to help couples work through all the basic areas of marital adjustment and to find positive principles for living. At the end of each chapter are practical assignments that stimulate communication and understanding. I suggest that a couple read a chapter each week and complete assignments individually and then dis-

> Marriages are not static. They are either growing or diminishing.

cuss assignments with each other. Many separated couples and couples in crisis are finding that process extremely beneficial in rebuilding their marriages.

For suggestions on restoring emotional love to a marriage, I strongly recommend *The 5 Love Languages*.[2] The book helps you identify the primary love language of your spouse. It is in speaking each other's love language that the emotional warmth of love returns. When we speak the other's love language, we communicate care and love. We also learn to fill each other's "love tank," which creates a climate for solving our conflicts and becoming friends again.

Many churches sponsor workshops and seminars on marriage as a part of their educational programs. Ask your pastor what is available in your church. Also, talk with Christian friends about what is available in their churches. Some church in your community likely has a program that would be of help to you as you seek to rebuild your marriage.

In reading a book or listening to a lecture on podcast, the value is not only in the ideas expressed but in the communication that they encourage. Couples should take notes as they listen and underline as they read and then tell each other what impressed them. As you talk to each other, seek to understand what your spouse is saying and feeling. Ask questions to clarify, such as, "Are you saying . . . ?" Repeat what you think your mate said and give him or her a chance to clarify. Express love even when you disagree. Remember, your objective in communication is to understand your spouse, to discover needs, and to find out how you can help meet those needs. If husband and wife concentrate on each other's fulfillment, it will not be long until your marriage will surpass your fondest dreams.

The growth patterns you established through counseling or reading, listening, and attending workshops must become a permanent part of your relationship. Marriages are not static. They are either growing or diminishing. You must continue to do the kind of things that stimulate growth. The ultimate goal is not a "perfect" marriage, but a "growing" marriage. Perfect is hard to define, and even if we reached it, perfection would be momentary. Growth is attainable today and every day. If you are growing there is hope, excitement, and fulfillment. Such growth should continue as long as you live. Thus, your marriage will always be alive.

Let your marriage relationship be the most important thing in your life. Give each other the number one place in your thoughts. Keep God at the center of your relationship. Do something each day to express your love for each other. Minimize the weaknesses of your mate and maximize his or her strengths. Brag about his accomplishments, and he will excel. Love, and you will be loved. Apply to your marriage the golden rule of all human relationships: "In everything, therefore, treat people the same way you want them to treat you" (Matthew 7:12 NASB).

GROWTH ASSIGNMENTS

1. No one, including God, will force you to work on your marriage. That is a decision that only you can make. But if you decide, you will have all the help of God at your disposal. You have talked with and observed many who have experienced divorce. Would you be

willing to find a couple that has a good marriage and ask them how they obtained it? Perhaps you could interview several married couples and ask what problems they have overcome to find fulfillment.

2. If you decide to take the road "less traveled by," you may want to use the checklist below:

Steps we have taken:	**Date:**

Made my decision to seek
reconciliation_____

Talked with God about my decision
and asked for His help_____

Asked my spouse for a
dinner date_____

Spouse accepted invitation_____

Related my decision to my spouse_____

Spouse agreed to seek reconciliation_____

Arranged for session with pastor or
counselor_____

Did assignments made by counselor_____

Additional counseling sessions_____

Completed additional communication
assignments_____

Additional counseling sessions_____

Completed additional communication
assignments_____

Books we have read and discussed:

1. _____

2. _____

3. _____

4. _____

5. _____

Podcasts or DVDs on marriage we have listened to and discussed:

1. _____

2. _____

3. _____

4. _____

5. _____

Marriage workshops, seminars, or classes we have attended:

1. _____

2. _____

3. _____

4. _____

5. _____

10

and if it doesn't work out . . .

Reconciliation is not always possible. Your best efforts may meet with coldness, hostility, and eventual failure. Even God was not always able to be reconciled to His people. "For all the adulteries of faithless Israel, I had sent her away and given her a writ of divorce" (Jeremiah 3:8 NASB). Reconciliation is not always possible because it requires the response of two people, and neither can force the other to return.

Human freedom is real. God would not force Israel to return. He put pressure on the nation by allowing its enemies to triumph. He removed His hand of blessing, but God did not force Israel to return. God will never remove man's freedom of choice. We must remember that as we pray. Many separated Christians have prayed and pleaded with God to "bring my spouse back." The spouse has not returned, so the Christian becomes discouraged and concludes that God does not answer prayer. Many have become hostile toward God and critical of the church and Christianity, and thus have turned from their only source of real help. But God will not force your spouse to return. He, in response to your prayers, will put pressure on him or her to seek reconciliation, but your spouse may still rebel against God's guidance and your best efforts.

Does the possibility of failure mean that we should not try? The whole teaching of the Bible stands in opposition to an attitude of futility. God never gives up on His people, and history is replete with examples of genuine spiritual restoration. Marital restoration is worth the risk of failure.

Your attitude is important. Don't say, "I might fail," but rather, "I might succeed!" Few goals are more deserving than the restoration of your marriage. If you can discover not what you had before the separation, but what you dreamed of having when you were married, your efforts will be rewarded. I have never met an individual who sincerely, consistently, and lovingly tried the things I suggest and regretted the effort. I have met scores of individuals who have succeeded and today are happily restored to their mates and growing with them.

> You cannot force reconciliation, because by its very nature reconciliation requires two people.

Throughout this book, I have tried to be realistic by indicating that you cannot control the response of your mate. You are the keeper of your own heart and responsible for your own words and actions. I have indicated that the biblical ideal calls you to seek reconciliation. You must face God with your willingness or refusal to pursue that ideal. Your spouse has the same responsibility. Your choice for reconciliation does not guarantee that your mate will reciprocate. He or she is free to choose.

Should I Contest Divorce?

If your mate demands divorce, there is little if anything to be gained by contesting such action. There was a time when most states required evidence of efforts at conciliation before a divorce would be granted. This is no longer true. Many counselors agree that forced efforts of reconciliation profit very little, because the blending of lives requires choice, not coercion. Divorce laws in most states are very liberal, and efforts at contesting the divorce result in little except expensive legal fees.

Contesting the divorce is simply a legal step in which one party seeks to prove that the other does not have grounds for divorce. That was feasible when state laws allowed for divorce only on the grounds of insanity, adultery, or abandonment. Today, however, with virtually all states having some form of no-fault divorce laws, such action at most only slows the process a bit. You may ask for time, and some states even require a separation of some months before divorce, but to seek to thwart divorce is futile.

It may seem unfair that if your spouse demands a divorce you have little choice except to go along with that choice, but such is the nature of human relationships. We cannot force anyone to be our friend. Friendship is a mutual choice between two people. If one chooses to dissolve the friendship, the other is helpless to keep it alive. Marriage is the most intimate of all friendships, and it too requires reciprocal action.

You cannot force reconciliation, because by its very nature

reconciliation requires two people. Divorce, however, which literally means "to disunite," requires only the action of one. If one person desires union and the other disunion, the one who desires disunion holds the upper hand, for union is impossible without his or her acquiescence.

Do I Need a Lawyer?

Divorce not only severs an emotional and physical relationship, but also a legal contract. Each state has its own laws and regulations regarding the dissolution of a marital contract. In most cases a lawyer will be needed to interpret the laws and guide in the process. In 1969 California initiated a no-attorney, no-court process for childless couples with no real estate, less than $5,000 in personal property, and less than $2,000 in debt. That streamlined divorce procedure cost only forty to fifty dollars in court fees. Forty-seven other states followed California's lead during the next twenty years.[1] Such no-fault divorce laws tend to award property equally to husband and wife, assuming that both will work and support themselves in the future.

With the passing of time, no-fault divorce laws proved to be unfair to women and children. In the late eighties, California made changes to correct this inequity, and other states have made or are making similar changes. Now, fault can be a factor in awarding property, child support, and alimony in most states. Because laws differ from state to state, most couples will need a lawyer to guide them in the legal aspects of divorce.

Do spouses need separate lawyers? If your spouse is divorcing you, his or her lawyer will be representing your spouse's interests. If you have had problems agreeing on finances, property, and child-related issues, then you will definitely need a lawyer to represent your interests. If you and your spouse can agree on an equitable settlement, then one attorney can represent both of you. Before you agree on one attorney, however, you should make a trip to the public library and read some of the many books and pamphlets on the legal aspects of divorce. You may also want to talk with several friends who have experienced divorce. That will give you a more realistic idea of what is involved in an equitable settlement.

Our emotions often get in the way of achieving a satisfactory settlement. Ann Diamond, a divorce lawyer, has listed the following situations in which emotions affect a fair settlement:

- A rejected spouse, unable to accept the finality of the separation, may agree to almost any demand of the other party in the hope that it will facilitate a reconciliation.
- A woman accustomed to having her husband make all important decisions will continue to look to him for advice, even though he has left her and is no longer interested in protecting her.
- The long-suffering, passive mate often seeks redress in the settlement for all past miseries of the relationship, whether self-inflicted or otherwise.
- When the breakup is sudden, the rejected spouse may be so traumatized that he, or more frequently she, is unable to make any realistic estimate of future financial need.
- The spouse who wants out may feel so guilty that he or she will try to compensate by being overly generous in property division and agreeing to pay or receive support

payments that are too high or too low. The subsequent resentment that can erupt over the long term will only cause further problems for both.

- Because the rejected partner may be too depressed to face any additional pressure, he or she will consent to any financial settlement just to get matters over with.
- One spouse may use the children as a means to punish and get even with the rejecting partner.[2]

You may need not only legal but emotional help in deciding upon the details of the settlement. As a Christian, you do not want to use the settlement as a punitive club on your spouse. On the other hand, you must be realistic about your needs and, if you have children, what is best for them.

What about the Children?

Tell children the truth about your separation and impending divorce. Don't try to protect them by lying. Eventually they will learn the truth, and if you have lied to them their confidence in you will be diminished. Simply, and with as little embellishment as possible, tell your children what has happened to your marriage. Ideally, both parents should talk with the children together and tell them their decision to divorce. Assure them of your love and tell them that they did not cause the divorce. If your spouse is not willing to join you in talking with the children, then you must do so alone and trust that your spouse will talk with them later.

It is extremely important that the child feel your love. The need to love and be loved is one of the strongest of all human emotions. In childhood, the need to be loved is related directly to the child's sense of security. Without love, the child will be emotionally insecure. Don't assume that your child feels loved simply because you tell him "I love you." The New Testament challenges us to love not in word only, but in deed (1 John 3:18). Find out what makes your child feel loved. For some children it is sitting close to them and talking; to others it is doing special things for them. Others feel loved when you give them unexpected gifts (that can also be used to exploit parents), whereas others respond to being held physically. Of course, you will want to say the words "I love you" frequently as well.[3]

Both parents should express love to the child in a way that the child understands. If one parent does not express love, however, there is little to be gained by the other parent's verbally assuring the child that the nonloving parent does love him. Actions speak louder than words to children. It is a cheap love whose only evidence is the word of someone else.

If a child says to the mother, "Daddy doesn't love me anymore, does he?" the thoughtful mother will respond, "Why do you say that, baby?" After the child has expressed disappointments, the mother might ask, "In what ways would you like Daddy to show his love to you?" The answer to that question should be communicated to the father, not in a condemning way, but as information. To the father or mother who has left I would say, "You have divorced your spouse. Please do not divorce your children. They need your love."

A second emotional need for the child is discipline. A child needs boundaries in order to feel secure. Sometimes a divorced parent will unconsciously try to make up for the child's loss by

> A common pitfall among divorced parents is that of allowing their own emotional needs to govern their actions toward the children.

indulging the child. If you give in to every wish of your child, you will soon be his servant, and he will grow up expecting others to serve him. The problem with a "king complex" (the feeling that everyone is expected to serve you) is that there are not many openings for kings in our society. The parent who raises a "king" is raising a misfit.

Your child needs the security of restrictions. If both parents can agree on basic patterns of conduct, so much the better. Such things as bedtime, study habits, screen time, what they eat, and general behavior can easily be agreed upon by parents who take seriously the task of raising a responsible child. When standards are different in the two places of residence, the child may enjoy the greater freedom granted by one parent, but he will lose the security of firm boundaries. If you cannot agree with your spouse on certain boundaries, then at least be consistent in your differences. Don't constantly change your rules. Such inconsistency is emotionally frustrating to the child.

A common pitfall among divorced parents is that of allowing their own emotional needs to govern their actions toward the children. For example, a parent might utilize exorbitant gift giving to win the love of the child and thus meet his own need to be loved. Or, one parent might constantly belittle the other in front of the child in order to vent hostility toward the ex-spouse. Such parading of each other's failures does not help the child. We must analyze our actions to ascertain their purpose. The well-being of the child must be the objective standard by which we judge our behavior.

In the early days of separation, the resident parent should seek to keep the children's routine as normal as possible. When feasible, the resident parent and children should remain in the house or apartment for at least several months. The divorce is traumatic enough. Moving to new surroundings, leaving friends, changing schools simply compound the feelings of insecurity in the child. If a move is necessary, try to maintain as many of the old established patterns of living as possible. Such things as reading stories, playing games, and praying together bring warm feelings even in a strange place.

The resident parent should welcome the involvement of the nonresident parent in the lives of the children. Most divorce settlements will give guidelines for the nonresident parent's time with the children. It is important to remember that both individuals are still parents, and though roles are changed, both should have ongoing relationships with the children. Exceptions to that may be when one parent is physically or emotionally unable to relate constructively to the children. This may be due to alcohol or drug abuse, physical or sexual abuse of the children, or mental incompetence. In such cases, the resident parent may want to seek counsel from a lawyer or counselor as to how to respond to the particular situation.

Friends, relatives, and the church family can be of inestimable value to the children of divorced parents. Grandfathers can serve as role models when the father, for whatever reason, is unable to spend time with children. Aunts and uncles are sometimes willing to have the children for extended visits. Friends may be able to spend quality time with the children and teach them specific skills. More and more churches are beginning to respond to the needs of the single parent. Workshops, seminars, books, and personal counseling are available in many churches. Don't hesitate to ask friends and relatives to help if you think they are capable of doing so. Many are willing, but will hesitate to take the initiative.

Living in a divorced home is not ideal for children, but then, much of life must be lived in a less than ideal setting. Be positive. Make the most of what you have. Put your hand in the hand of God; reach out for available help. Let the love of God comfort you and the power of God enable you to be the best possible single parent.

Am I Free to Remarry?

It is beyond the scope of this book to give a lengthy treatise of the biblical passages dealing with divorce and remarriage. A number of excellent books are available that give a detailed exegetical analysis of those passages.[4] The Bible emphasizes God's ideal: monogamous marriage for life. It speaks of divorce as humans' failure to experience the ideal, but it says very little about remarriage.

Even in the case of widows and widowers, the Bible neither commands nor forbids remarriage. The choice is left to the individual as he or she seeks to discern what is best for them (Romans 7:1–6; 1 Corinthians 7:6–9; 1 Timothy 5:14). In the case of divorce because of fornication or desertion, again the Bible is silent about remarriage. Thus, in the case of divorce because of fornication or desertion, many believe the Bible does not condemn or commend remarriage.

Divorce does take place for reasons other than sexual unfaithfulness and desertion, however. With the rise of no-fault divorce laws, most divorces grow out of very subjective reasons, like supposed incompatibility. Remarriage of those divorced for causes other than fornication and desertion constitutes adultery, according to the statements of Jesus and Paul.[5] Paul says in 1 Corinthians 7:10–11 (NASB), "To the married I give instructions, not I, but the Lord, that the wife should not leave her husband (but if she does leave, she must remain unmarried, or else be reconciled to her husband), and that the husband should not divorce his wife."

Most counselors agree that it takes about two years to work through the emotional trauma of a divorce.

Although the possibility of divorce is recognized, it is never encouraged in Scripture. Remarriage, except possibly when the divorce is based upon fornication or desertion, is always seen as adultery. Immediately, the question is raised, cannot adultery be forgiven? The answer is clearly yes. If there is genuine confession of sin, adultery can be forgiven.

Forgiveness, however, does not erase all the results of sin. Thousands of forgiven couples will testify of the ever-present scars that are never fully erased.

Should you remarry? Why not put that question on the shelf until you have made every effort at reconciliation? If reconciliation is impossible—if the divorce is finalized, if your spouse has remarried or has been sexually unfaithful and refuses all attempts at reconciliation—you may consider remarriage. But do not move too fast. Most counselors agree that it takes about two years to work through the emotional trauma of a divorce. Premature remarriage is tempting—but risky. That perhaps accounts for the fact that the divorce rate of second marriages is higher than that of first marriages. Take more time to prepare for your second marriage. Unity will be more difficult to obtain because of the frustrations and memories you bring to the second marriage. Rediscover yourself before you seek remarriage.

GROWTH ASSIGNMENTS

1. If your spouse insists on divorce and refuses to take any steps toward reconciliation, ask God to give you strength and wisdom in accepting this decision.
2. Keep the door of reconciliation open from your side and pray that God will continue to stimulate the mind of your spouse.
3. Seek the counsel of a lawyer, a pastor, or a friend in the areas in which you have questions.
4. Seek to be equitable in all legal arrangements.

5. Select one or more of the books or websites from the resources listed in the resources list at the end of this book, and continue seeking personal growth.

11

facing the
future

Contrary to your present feelings, your future can be bright. God's plans for you are good. " 'For I know the plans I have for you,' says the Lord. 'They are plans for good and not for disaster, to give you a future and a hope' " (Jeremiah 29:11).

Past failures need not destroy your hope for the future. If you choose, you can discover the elation of a marriage reborn— reborn on a much deeper level than before. Your communication and understanding of each other can be much more intimate than you have ever known. As you forgive the past, share feelings, find understanding, and learn to love each other, you can find fulfillment in your marriage. That is not wishful thinking. It has become reality for hundreds of couples who have committed themselves to walk the road to reconciliation.

I have tried to be realistic as I have described the process of restoring a marriage. It is not easy. It will be painful as your mate communicates honest feelings that have developed through the years. You will have the tendency to defend yourself and deny that you have not met needs. You will see clearly the failures of your spouse whereas your own will seem insignificant. It is hard to admit that you have also failed your spouse.

As both of you understand your failures and move to correct them, you can experience tremendous personal growth. Some of the things you have disliked about yourself through the years can be changed. You are not a slave to old patterns of behavior. You will be greatly encouraged as you see yourself becoming the loving, thoughtful person you want to be. You will be excited about the positive changes you see in your spouse.

Such change is not likely to happen without the help of God. You both need to return to God in a fresh way. If you have not done so, you may want to invite Christ into your life. Jesus died to pay the penalty for your past sins. God wants to forgive. He will not hold the past against you, if you will accept Christ as your Savior. The Spirit of God will come to live with you and give you power to make needed changes in your life. With His help, you can accomplish things you never dreamed possible. Your whole life can be turned around, and in turn you can help others.

I want to challenge you to accept God's forgiveness, open the door of your life to Christ, and with your hand in God's hand move out to attempt the things suggested in this book. You will never regret your attempts to accomplish God's best.

As I have tried to say throughout this book, your efforts do not guarantee the restoration of your marriage. Your spouse has the freedom to turn away from all your overtures. If, after you make every effort at reconciliation, your spouse refuses to be reconciled, where does that leave you? It leaves you with your hand in God's hand. That is not a bad position. You will be free from the guilt of past failures, because you will have confessed your wrong to God and to your spouse. You will have the satisfaction of having sought reconciliation. Your relationship with God will be vital and growing. You will appreciate your own abilities and admit your weaknesses. You will be on a program of personal growth and ministry that will lead to fulfillment. God will not hold you responsible for the decision of your spouse. You are only responsible for your own attitudes and behavior.

If reconciliation is not possible, do not think that God's purposes for you are over. God has gifted you and called you to serve in His family. He wants to use your life for positive purposes, and He wants to meet all of your needs (Philippians 4:19). Don't say, "I can never be happy without my spouse." If your spouse will not return, God will still lead you from the valley of despair to the mountain of joy. God is not through with you. Your happiness is not dependent upon the behavior of your spouse, but upon your response to God and life. "For God is working in you, giving you the desire and the power to do what pleases him" (Philippians 2:13).

The highest goal in life is to follow God's leadership daily. God will not only show you the way to walk, but He will give the power to take the necessary steps. He will use friends, His church, and quality resources to help you. In those hours when no one else can help, He will assure you of His presence. As David said, "You will make known to me the path of life; in Your presence is fullness of joy; in Your right hand there are pleasures forever" (Psalm 16:11 NASB).

In the privacy of our own hearts, no one can ever destroy the deep peace that is the result of knowing God as Father. Nothing could bring more security. No human relationship can replace our need for sharing life with God. He in turn will lead us in developing human relationships in which we can love and be loved by others.

The future is intended to be the brightest portion of your life. I would encourage you to say with the psalmist, "This is the day the Lord has made. We will rejoice and be glad in it" (Psalm 118:24). You may not be able to rejoice over the past or even over your present situation, but you can rejoice that God has given you the ability to use this day for good. When you do, you will be glad.

Notes

Introduction: "I Can't Take It Anymore"

1. Samuel Rainey, email, November 2013.

Chapter 1: What Happened to Our Dream?

1. Gary Chapman, *Desperate Marriages* (Chicago: Northfield, 2008), 34.
2. See Leviticus 21:14, 22:13; Numbers 30:9; Deuteronomy 24:1–4.
3. Gary Smalley, *Winning Your Wife Back Before It's Too Late* (Nashville: Thomas Nelson, 2004), 101.

Chapter 2: How to Start Saving Your Marriage

1. Ed Wheat, *How to Save Your Marriage Alone* (Grand Rapids: Zondervan, 1983).
2. Michelle Weiner-Davis, *Divorce Busting* (New York: Simon & Schuster, 1992), 27.
3. Judy Bodmer, "My Loveless Marriage," *Today's Christian Woman*, http://www.todayschristianwoman.com/articles/2006/january/14.46.html.
4. Gary Smalley, *Winning Your Wife Back Before It's Too Late* (Nashville: Thomas Nelson, 2004), 27.
5. Michael J. McManus, *Marriage Savers* (Grand Rapids: Zondervan, 1993), 28.
6. See Judith Wallerstein and Sandra Blakeslee, *Second Chances: Men, Women, and Children a Decade After Divorce, Who Wins, Who Loses—and Why* (New York: Ticknor & Fields, 1989).
7. Michelle Weiner-Davis, 21.
8. Britton Wood, *Single Adults Want to Be the Church, Too* (Nashville: Broadman, 1977), 82.

Chapter 5: Love Is . . .

1. Gary Smalley, *Winning Your Wife Back Before It's Too Late* (Nashville: Thomas Nelson, 2004), 33.
2. Michelle Weiner-Davis, *Divorce Busting* (New York: Simon & Schuster, 1992), 75.

Chapter 6: Tough Love

1. Robert Frost, "Mending Wall," ed. Edward Conery Lathem, *The Poetry of Robert Frost* (New York: Holt, Rinehart and Winston, 1969).

Chapter 7: Loneliness: "The Deepest Pit"

1. Email, November 2013.
2. James J. Lynch in an interview with Christopher Anderson, *People*, 22 August 1977, 30.
3. Maya Pines, "Psychological Hardness: The Role of Challenge in Health," *Psychology Today*, December 1980, 43.
4. "Divorce," *Christian Medical Society Journal* 7, no. 1 (Winter 1976): 30.
5. Robert S. Weiss, *The Experience of Emotional and Social Isolation* (Cambridge: Massachusetts Institute of Technology, 1973), 54.
6. Ibid., 57.
7. James Johnson, *Loneliness Is Not Forever* (Chicago: Moody, 1979), 21.
8. Paul Tournier, *Escape from Loneliness* (Philadelphia: Westminster, 1976), 23.

Chapter 9: Rebuilding

1. Robert Frost, "The Road Not Taken," ed. Edward Conery Lathem, *The Poetry of Robert Frost* (New York: Holt, Rinehart and Winston, 1969).
2. Gary Chapman, *The 5 Love Languages* (Chicago: Northfield, 2010).

Chapter 10: And If It Doesn't Work Out . . .

1. Michael J. McManus, *Marriage Savers* (Grand Rapids: Zondervan, 1993), 230.
2. Mel Krantzler, *Creative Divorce* (New York: New American Library, 1975), 220.
3. For a fuller discussion of how to discover your child's primary love language, read Gary Chapman and Ross Campbell, *The 5 Love Languages of Children* (Chicago: Northfield, 2012).
4. See H. Wayne House, *Divorce and Remarriage: Four Christian Views* (Downers Grove, IL: InterVarsity, 1990).
5. See Matthew 5:32, 19:9; Mark 10:11–12; Luke 16:18; 1 Corinthians 7:15.

resources

Whether you are able to move down the road of reconciliation, or you are forced to accept divorce, reading the right books and exploring helpful Internet content can be a tremendous aid in helping you make the most of life. You may not agree with all you read, but look for practical ideas that may assist you in accomplishing your goals. God has not left us without direction. Books written from a biblical perspective can help you find God's way. Remember, it is not enough just to read. You must apply truth to life. You may need to make radical changes in your present thinking and behavior. If so, you have all of God's power to aid you.

RESOURCES FOR GROWING WHILE SEPARATED

Carder, Dave, with Duncan Jaenicke. *Torn Asunder: Recovering from Extramarital Affairs*. Chicago: Moody, 2007. There is hope for recovery from the devastation of extramarital affairs. This book offers practical counsel for beginning the recovery process. Carder analyzes why affairs happen and provides step-by-step help for recovering and rebuilding.

_____. *Torn Asunder Workbook*. Chicago: Moody, 2008. This workbook applies the principles in the original *Torn*

Asunder with a series of projects and responses that can bring healing to the wounds created by marital unfaithfulness.

Chapman, Gary. *Anger: Handling a Powerful Emotion in a Healthy Way*. Chicago: Moody, 2007. Anger can be productive and generate positive change if it is valid and expressed in a constructive manner. But how do you know the difference between valid and distorted anger? And how can you use anger to effectively build up a personal relationship rather than tear it down? The book answers these questions and offers practical suggestions for controlling your anger so it does not control you.

Clinton, Tim, and Gary Sibcy. *Why You Do the Things You Do: The Secret to Healthy Relationships*. Brentwood, Tenn.: Integrity Publishers, 2006. There is no one person who feels, acts, and thinks exactly like you. Dr. Tim Clinton and Dr. Gary Sibcy present four patterns of relating that help explain why you do the things you do, and how your behaviors are rooted in your past and specifically in your bond with your parents. Learning this information about yourself will help you see how it affects and can improve your relationships.

Cloud, Henry, and John Townsend. *Boundaries in Marriage: Understanding the Choices That Make or Break Loving Relationships*. Grand Rapids, Mich.: Zondervan, 2002. Authors of the bestselling *Boundaries* present the ten laws of boundaries that can make a tremendous difference both in marriage and in relationships in general.

McGinnis, Alan Loy. *The Friendship Factor: How to Get Closer to the People You Care For*. Minneapolis: Augsburg, 2004. This book is a must for couples who want to become friends. It is filled with ideas on how to deepen relationships, cultivate intimacy, handle negative emotions, and forgive. The section on salvaging a faltering friendship has particular application to those who are separated.

Rooks, Linda. *Broken Heart on Hold: Surviving Separation*. Elgin, Ill.: David C. Cook Publishing, 2006. Written by a woman who has gone through the pain of marital separation and come out on the other side with a stronger, reconciled marriage, this book has the power to encourage, comfort, and give hope to those who are in a similar situation. Providing biblical insight along the way, Linda Rooks reminds the reader that God is still there and should be trusted.

Scruggs, Jeff, and Cheryl Scruggs. *I Do Again: How We Found a Second Chance at Our Marriage—and You Can Too*. Colorado Springs: WaterBrook Press, 2008. Jeff and Cheryl Scruggs share their story of a happy beginning, a downward spiral, a traumatic affair, and a painful divorce that left their family in pieces. Jeff and Cheryl share the secrets of what was really going wrong in their marriage before the divorce, and also take the reader on their journey to reconciliation and eventual remarriage. Their story proves what God is able to do by His grace with two forgiving hearts.

Talley, Jim. *Reconcilable Differences: Healing for Troubled Marriages*. Nashville: Nelson, 1991, 2008. Are our differences too great to be reconciled? Talley believes the answer is no. The goal of reconciliation is to cause those who are angry, bitter, and hostile to become friendly again and to discover harmony. The book offers practical help on resolving conflicts and developing a relationship based on mutual love, respect, and trust.

RESOURCES FOR REBUILDING A MARRIAGE

Begg, Alistair. *Lasting Love: How to Avoid Marital Failure.* Chicago: Moody, 1997, 2002. When marriages are shaky, couples need to return to the biblical basics, such as understanding the meaning of the marriage vows. This book includes a helpful study guide that couples can complete together.

Chapman, Gary, and Ramon Presson. *101 Conversation Starters for Couples.* Chicago: Northfield, 2002, 2012. One hundred and one questions are listed in this small and fun booklet to help couples "disclose and discover"—both key elements to creating or restoring intimacy in marriage.

Chapman, Gary, and Jennifer Thomas. *When Sorry Isn't Enough: Making Things Right with Those You Love.* Chicago: Northfield, 2013. No matter what state your marriage is in, rocky or solid, everyone eventually does something they regret. This book walks you through the different forms of apologies and why one "method" may be more meaningful to your spouse than another. Discover how the power of apology can heal your relationships and bring great rewards to your marriage.

Chapman, Gary. *Desperate Marriages: Moving Toward Hope and Healing in Your Relationship.* Chicago: Northfield, 2008. A marriage can come under fire from alcoholism, verbal abuse, a controlling personality, or unfaithfulness. This book shows how to deal with these and other "tough issues."

_____. *The 5 Love Languages*. Chicago: Northfield, 2010. What makes one person feel loved does not necessarily make another feel loved. The key to keeping love alive in a marriage is discovering the primary love language of your spouse and choosing to speak it regularly. Dr. Chapman describes each of the five love languages and gives guidance for applying these principles in marriage. Includes self-assessments.

_____. *The Marriage You've Always Wanted*. Chicago: Moody, 2014. Once you make the decision to seek reconciliation, this book will point the way toward marital growth. Dr. Chapman covers such key issues as finances, sex, communication, and much more, emphasizing the importance of marital unity. Each chapter concludes with specific "growth assignments" so spouses may act on what they've learned.

Dobson, James. *Love Must Be Tough: New Hope for Marriages in Crisis*. Carol Stream, Ill.: Tyndale, 2007. This book is for spouses who have tried numerous strategies and offered many second chances. Dr. James Dobson offers hope to those who are close to walking away, sharing a new way to love their mate, even if they are the only ones willing to give the marriage another try.

Downs, Tim, and Joy Downs. *Fight Fair: Winning at Conflict Without Losing at Love*. Chicago: Moody, 2010. Conflict is "the art of disagreeing while still holding hands," and the authors remind every married couple that conflict is part of marriage and of life that they cannot escape. Readers learn to establish their own rules of engagement and to employ the appropriate underlying attitudes, which include humility, generosity, and gentleness.

_____. *One of Us Must Be Crazy . . . And I'm Pretty Sure It's You: Making Sense of the Differences That Divide Us.* Chicago: Moody, 2010. This companion book to *Fight Fair* presents the seven areas where most conflicts occur and prescribes how to resolve each conflict when alienation has set in.

Gottman, John, PhD, and Nan Silver. *What Makes Love Last?* New York: Simon & Schuster, 2012. Drawing on decades of research, psychologist and counselor Gottman looks at why some marriages thrive and some wither, and explores the central role of trust.

Leman, Kevin. *Sheet Music.* Carol Stream, Ill.: Tyndale, 2003. With typical candor, Kevin Leman tells couples everything they need to know about building a healthy and rewarding sexual relationship. He looks at attitudes, techniques, and much more.

Penner, Clifford, and Joyce Penner. *The Gift of Sex.* Nashville: W Publishing, 2003. One of the most comprehensive and practical guides to discovering mutual sexual fulfillment in a marriage, this book deals realistically with common struggles and frustrations. It speaks to the most often asked questions of couples who want to find sexual harmony.

Smalley, Gary, with Dr. Greg Smalley and Deborah Smalley. *Winning Your Wife Back Before It's Too Late.* Nashville: Thomas Nelson, 1999, 2004. The veteran relationships expert addresses men whose marriages are in crisis—

"whether she's left physically or emotionally." Combines straight talk, Scripture, and humor, presented in a "game plan" theme.

Weiner-Davis, Michelle. *Divorce Busting*. New York: Simon & Schuster, 1992. A marriage therapist offers practical, tough-minded help for couples "on the brink"—and reflects on the reasons why divorce is not the answer.

Williams, Joe, and Michelle Williams. *Yes, Your Marriage Can Be Saved*. Carol Stream, Ill.: Tyndale, 2007. A Focus on the Family book. The authors share insights gleaned from their journey through separation and reconciliation.

RESOURCES FOR COPING WITH DIVORCE

Birdseye, Sue. *When Happily Ever After Shatters: Seeing God in the Midst of Divorce & Single Parenting*. Colorado Springs: Focus on the Family, 2013. When your marriage has failed, it's easy to turn to bitterness and despair. Sue Birdseye shows you another route: turning to God, and trusting and honoring Him even in the midst of divorce. Sharing her own story along the way, Sue provides practical advice in areas such as single parenting, forgiveness, and bringing glory to God even in the hardest of circumstances.

Burns, Bob, and Tom Whiteman. *The Fresh Start Divorce Recovery Workbook*. Nashville: Oliver Nelson, 1998. A step-by-step program for those who are divorced or separated, this book points the way to healing. Questions, self-tests, exercises, and practical information will enable readers to regain self-esteem and faith in God; move beyond bitterness and anger into forgiveness and spiritual freedom; help children handle adjustments; and gain personal strength to complete the journey toward wholeness after the trauma of divorce.

Kniskern, Joseph Warren. *When the Vow Breaks: A Survival and Recovery Guide for Christians Facing Divorce.* Nashville: B&H, 2008. A survival and recovery guide for Christians facing divorce. In this sensitive and thorough guide, attorney Joseph Kniskern describes the walk through the emotional aspects of his own failed marriage and unwanted divorce. He provides a comprehensive study of what the Bible says about marriage and divorce. More importantly, he shows how God can and does continue to work in people's lives to provide hope and encouragement in the aftermath of a divorce.

Petherbridge, Laura. *When I Do Becomes I Don't: Practical Steps During Separation and Divorce.* Elgin, Ill.: David C. Cook Publishing, 2008. There are many concerns in the midst of a separation or divorce, and it can be difficult to find practical answers in the midst of the pain. Laura Petherbridge asks the hard questions and gives helpful answers to areas such as identity, finances, forgiveness, singleness, legal issues, returning to work, criticism, and trusting God.

Smoke, Jim. *Growing Through Divorce.* Irvine, Calif.: Harvest House, 2007. When reconciliation is impossible and divorce a reality, this book points the way to life beyond divorce. This very practical book deals with such subjects as assuming responsibility for yourself, finding a family, finding forgiveness, your children, your future, and new life.

_____. *Moving Forward: A Devotional Guide for Finding Hope and Peace in the Midst of Divorce.* Peabody,

Mass.: Hendrickson, 2000. Drawing from his years of counseling experience, Smoke offers day-by-day devotions that explore—from a positive and compassionate point of view—the issues confronting those going through divorce. With words of en-couragement and understanding, the book addresses feelings of loneliness, insecurity, anxiety, and anger. It offers insight on issues of forgiveness, children, hope, and peace in the midst of divorce.

ONLINE RESOURCES

5LoveLanguages.com: Advice and resources on relationship issues from world-renowned author, speaker, and counselor Dr. Gary Chapman. Also features the 30-second assessment tool for determining your love language.

CloudTownsend.com: Drs. Henry Cloud and John Townsend offer a wealth of resources particular to couples struggling in their marriage, including free advice, videos, articles, upcoming and online workshops and events, and online coaching.

DivorceCare.org: DivorceCare groups meet weekly for a time of support with other adults going through divorce. Top experts address divorce and recovery topics. There is also time to discuss the topics as a group and hear what is going on in the lives of the other group members. This website provides a search tool to find a local group.

FocusontheFamily.com: An abundance of resources on many areas and issues pertaining to marriage, family, divorce, and separation.

HomeWord.com: HomeWord, partner of Azusa Pacific University, provides a wealth of information to strengthen and encourage couples and families, including material covering marriage, divorce, adultery, separation, and parenting.

acknowledgments

I am deeply indebted to the many individuals who have shared their struggles with me. Out of the midst of the ambivalent feelings of love and hate, anger and concern, many of them have pursued the high road of reconciliation. Not all have succeeded, but all have matured. I have watched them deal responsibly with failure and rise to face the future with confidence. Their example has served to encourage me in the writing of this volume, which is designed to point the way to hope.

Sincere appreciation is expressed to Betsey Newenhuyse who served as the editor on this project. The entire Moody Publishers team has been extremely supportive in this effort to help couples give their relationship *One More Try*.

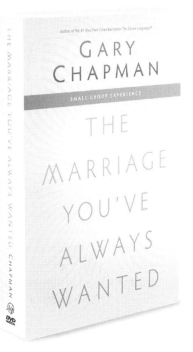

Broken down into five 45-60 minute sessions for small group study, *The Marriage You've Always Wanted Small Group Experience* gives couples the essential tools they need to improve and enrich or prepare for marriage. Utilizing DVD clips from Dr. Gary Chapman's widely popular conference series, small groups will dive deep into discussions regarding key topics such as:

- Communication 101
- Understanding and expressing love
- Initiating positive change
- Making sex a mutual joy
- How to share the things that bug you

*This five-session curriculum includes one DVD, a group leader's guide, and a participant workbook (containing five weeks of bonus devotions). *Additional copies of the small group workbook are available to order separately for $9.99.*

VISIT CHAPMANLIVE.COM

WHEN SORRY ISN'T ENOUGH: MAKING THINGS RIGHT WITH THOSE YOU LOVE

In this book, you'll discover new and healthy ways to effectively approach and mend fractured relationships. Even better, you'll discover how meaningful apologies provide the power to make your friendships, family, and marriage stronger than ever before.

ANGER: TAMING A POWERFUL EMOTION

In *Anger*, Dr. Gary Chapman offers helpful (and sometimes surprising) insights into why you get angry and what you can do about it. Using real-life examples of transformed lives and relationships, Chapman explains how to: recognize the difference between "bad" and "good" anger, use anger to motivate you toward positive change, release long-simmering resentment, and teach others (like your children) how to deal with anger.

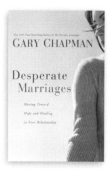

DESPERATE MARRIAGES: MOVING TOWARDS HOPE AND HEALING IN YOUR RELATIONSHIP

You never thought your marriage would come to this. Now the one thing you don't see coming is hope. As bad as it may seem, help can be on the way and a peaceful resolution can be closer than you think. Renowned marriage counselor Gary Chapman provides positive steps for dealing with the most deeply rooted wounds.

AVAILABLE WHEREVER BOOKS ARE SOLD.